Faith is one those key elements in life that you really cannot afford to live without. It is the only way to bring ultimate pleasure to God. In Jack Coe's *40 Days to Faith,* you will be taken on a journey into an entirely new dimension, the dimension called faith. In this realm you will begin to experience life like you have never realized it before. Using personal stories from his battle with cancer, Coe will show you step-by-step how to defeat any giant that may rise up against you by employing age-old principles that work. Brother Coe has already done it, and so can you.

—Bishop LeRoy Bailey, Jr.
Senior Pastor of The First Cathedral
Presiding Prelate of Churches Covered
and Connected in Covenant
Author of *A Solid Foundation*

I have known Brother Coe for nearly ten years. In that time I have learned a great deal from him about exercising my faith in God. Most people who battle cancer as severely as he has never live to tell their story. Not so with Brother Coe. God has resurrected him from the hands of death for the sole purpose of being able to share his victorious testimony. The very essence of this marvelous work is to show you that no matter how impossible your problem may appear to be right now, with God all things are truly possible—if only you believe. Great food to feed your faith!

—Pastor Aaron D. Lewis
Pastor of The Family of God
Author of *Keys to Unlocking Your Destiny* and
Healing for the 21st Century

From the first time Jack Coe visited our church and ministered, I knew instantly that we would have him back again and again. He ministered on the subject of faith in such a practical way that the members of our congregation instantly began to apply what they had learned to produce tangible results in their lives. I cannot even count the amount of times that he has come to our church, yet each time faith deposits are made and great harvests are reaped. *40 Days to Faith* can be considered the book version of his faith teachings. In the same way that harvest comes after the Word has been sown, expect to reap an abundant harvest after reading this work.

—Dr. Earl Johnson
Senior Pastor of Covenant Life Church

40 DAYS TO FAITH

JACK COE, JR.

WHITAKER
HOUSE

---

40 DAYS TO FAITH

Jack Coe Ministries
P.O. Box 398538
Dallas, TX 75339
website: jackcoe.org
e-mail: jackcoe1@aol.com

ISBN: 0-88368-960-X
Printed in the United States of America
© 2004 by Jack Coe, Jr.

Whitaker House
30 Hunt Valley Circle
New Kensington, PA 15068
website: www.whitakerhouse.com

Library of Congress Cataloging-in-Publication Data
Coe, Jack, 1944–
40 days to faith / by Jack Coe, Jr.
p. cm.
ISBN 0-88368-960-X (trade pbk. : alk. paper)
1. Faith. I. Title: Forty days to faith. II. Title.
BV4637.C565 2004
234'.23—dc22
2004015248

1 2 3 4 5 6 7 8 9 10 **ɰ** 10 09 08 07 06 05 04

CONTENTS

INTRODUCTION

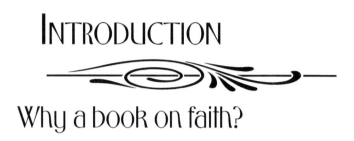

Why a book on faith?

aith. Consider with me, for a minute, what a versatile little word *faith* is. Aside from its popularity as a woman's name, it can be used

- to delineate denominational or religious differences, as in, "He's of a different *faith* than me";
- to express encouragement, as in, "I have *faith* that you can ace your test at school today";
- to voice wistful optimism, as in, "I'm putting my *faith* in you, so please don't drop me as you're lifting me over this fence";
- or to convey deep-held convictions or beliefs, as in, "I put my faith in God."

As you can see, there's a whole lot packed into this tiny, five-letter, single-syllable word. This list is by no means exhaustive, either. *Faith* has significance on many different levels, yet frequently we just gloss over it, paying little to no attention as to how the word is being used. In the list above, for instance, someone could easily say, "I put my faith in God," yet deep down really mean nothing more than, "I hope there is a God out there who will come through for me when all's said and done." Unless we're careful to communicate exactly what we mean by *faith,*

it's easy to presume someone's on the same plane as us when, in fact, he or she might be stuck on the level of "wistful optimism," while we're at the level of "deep-held convictions."

In order to avoid any misunderstandings, it's my goal in this book to start with the basics and build from there. Before we can delve into the faith's depths, we have to "suit up" for the dive. Part of that suiting up process includes coming to a consensus on what the word *faith* even means. We'll do this in the book's opening chapters.

Once we've suited up, we'll be ready to delve deeper into faith—specifically, Christian faith—and all that it entails. The Bible will serve as our guidebook for this part of the dive since it is here, in God's Word, that faith is most perfectly defined—and even demonstrated, through the life of Jesus Christ our Lord.

God has blessed me with some amazing faith-stretching experiences, and I would be foolish to omit them. From struggling with my father's death to facing my own battle against what was supposed to be terminal cancer, I've had my share of tests and trials. Looking back, I am grateful for these experiences, for I can see how the Lord strengthened my faith through them.

Faith doesn't come overnight. Quite honestly, it probably can't even be mastered in forty days! I'm still growing in faith and, by God's grace, will still be growing until the day He takes me home to be with him. While this book won't *give* you perfect faith—only the Holy Spirit can do that—it's my prayer that it will give you a better understanding of perfect faith. For until we understand what we're seeking after, we cannot truly pursue it.

May God guide you as you grow in faith!

God bless,
Jack Coe, Jr.

Day One

Faith, at a basic level, is simply belief.

God has dealt to each one a measure of faith.
—Romans 12:3

You'd have to be blind and deaf to think that Christians are popular these days. Turn on any news program, any television show, any late night movie, and you'll probably get a pretty derogatory representation of Christians. Usually Christians are portrayed as narrow-minded, fanatical, unloving, old-fashioned, and sometimes downright ignorant. Consequently, when most people in our society hear "Christian" or "believer" or "person of faith," that is precisely what comes to mind: a narrow-minded, fanatical, unloving, old-fashioned, and downright ignorant dinosaur.

Why is this? A big reason is that our culture has developed what could be called the "Missouri mentality." Just as Florida is "The Sunshine State" and Texas is "The Lone Star State," Missouri is "The Show-Me State." People with the Missouri mentality are always demanding proof. "When I

see it, I'll believe it," they say. There's nothing wrong with wanting proof, but this mentality has so permeated our society that an overzealous, unhealthy skepticism has been born. "If it can't be scientifically proven," the skeptic says, "it can't be trusted."

I'd like to challenge this way of thinking. I'd like to suggest that *every single person in this world*—"show it to me" skeptics included—is a "person of faith." Now, don't go hanging me for heresy because you think I just said everyone in the world is a saved Christian bound for heaven. That's not what I'm saying. What I mean is simply this: *Everyone has faith.* Period. Even the most skeptical of skeptics has faith in *something.* As such, every single person in this world is a person of faith because *everybody believes in something.*

"But, Jack," you say, "I know some people who don't believe in *anything.* What about those who consider themselves to be agnostics? What about atheists? How can you call them people of faith?"

Ah, but they *do* believe in *some*thing, as we'll see in a moment, and that means that they have faith. But before we go much further, let's establish what we mean by "faith." *Merriam-Webster's New Collegiate Dictionary* contains several different definitions for the word *faith.* The one that most people are familiar with is "belief and trust in and loyalty to God; belief in the traditional doctrines of a religion." This is what most people think of when they hear the word *faith.*

Closely related to this definition, however, is the one that immediately follows. It reads, "Firm belief in something for which there is no proof; complete trust." This is the kind of "faith" I'm talking about when I say that everyone is a person

of faith. In other words, all people make decisions based on beliefs for which they have no absolute proof. No matter what you believe, no matter how scientific and "provable" it might seem, it still takes faith to accept it. Even the simple act of accepting that your proof is accurate and indeed "proof" takes faith.

Let's look at a very basic example. When we lay down in our beds at night, we are operating in faith, for we *trust* and *believe* that the bed will hold us and not collapse; if we're not operating by that faith—in other words, if we're not sure that the bed will actually hold our weight—then we probably won't climb on top of the bed. (At least I hope we won't!)

"But, Jack," you say, "it can be scientifically proven if a bed will hold a person's weight or not. How is that faith? I thought faith was something for which there was no proof!"

Ah, but remember, proof takes faith. Even if proof can be proven by more proof—and that proof by more proof, and that proof by more proof, etc., etc., etc.— there's still proof somewhere along the line that is going to require faith.

> Every single person is a person of faith.

Having faith in a bed, for instance, takes faith in physics, which takes faith in the orderly arrangement and behavior of nature. Now, I'm no engineer or physicist, and I don't pretend to be, but I understand a little bit about how things are put together. For instance, I know that water is sometimes called H_2O, meaning that the smallest amount of water you can get would consist of two hydrogen atoms and one oxygen atom. Now, when you go to pour yourself a glass of water from a pitcher in the refrigerator, you know that water

will come out of that pitcher. How do you know? Because, from experience, you know that water always comes out of the water pitcher. You put water into it, and you expect to get water out of it.

Now I'm going to get a little goofy on you, but stay with me. Imagine that, for some strange reason, the hydrogen atoms got sick of being hydrogen atoms and decided it was time for a makeover. After thinking it over a bit, they decided, "Nitrogen sounds good," and so they turned themselves into nitrogen atoms all by themselves. Do you know what would happen? You wouldn't have water anymore—you'd have a pitcher full of laughing gas!

What if a similar thing happened in our wooden bed example? What if, right before you were to lie down on it, all the atoms in that bed decided to rearrange and mix things up a bit so that, in the end, the wooden bed frame turned into a flimsy structure of straw. Would you want to lie down on that bed? I don't think so! It would fall straight to the floor in no time flat.

You see, when you go to pour a glass of water or lie down on a bed, you are exhibiting *faith*—faith that the tiny particles inside that water and inside that wood are going to continue behaving as they have for all time. To go back to our definition, faith is a "firm belief in something for which there is no proof," and that's exactly what we have in the water and wood examples. Can we prove beyond a shadow of a doubt that water and wood will never go crazy like this? No! How can we prove something that has not happened? We must simply trust, in faith, that the proof we do have thus far—that water and wood typically keep their identities as water and wood unless something interferes with them—is true.

Day One

The nineteenth-century humorist Josh Billings said it well. "If there was no faith," he wrote, "there would be no living in this world. We couldn't even eat hash with safety."[*] As Billings so cleverly expressed, even the most basic and obvious of "facts" has a step of faith at its core. So the next time someone criticizes you for being a silly, old-fashioned, ignorant ole person of faith, remind him that he himself— even with his skepticism, experimental proofs, and show-it-to-me mentality—is a person of faith, as well. Remind him, too, that his beliefs in the certainty of science are just as subject to the same strict standards of criticism that he uses to judge your belief in the infallibility of God's Word.

---

[*] Josh Billings, *His Complete Works* (1888). <http://www.quotegarden.com/faith.html> (6 June 2004)

Day Two

Faith is only as good as its object.

I don't know how many times you've heard it, but I've probably heard it a thousand times: "It doesn't matter what you have faith in, as along as you have faith in something." Unlike the skeptics we discussed in the last chapter, people who think like this are not afraid to admit that they believe in something, that they have faith. What they *are* afraid of is making judgment calls. You'll never hear them say, "You should be careful what you believe in, because what you believe in and base your life upon might be wrong." Instead, they throw all caution and sound reasoning to the wind. "Believe in anything," they say, "as long as you believe in it sincerely, you'll be fine." Sincerity is all that really matters in these folks' minds.

I'm sure the people on the Titanic wish that sincerity was all that really mattered. Most of the people on that "unsinkable" ship in 1912, passengers and crew members alike, sincerely believed the Titanic could not be sunk. Titanic survivor Lawrence Beesley showed this in his book *Loss of the S.S. Titanic.* He wrote,

The history of the R.M.S. Titanic, of the White Star Line, is one of the most tragically short it is possible to conceive. The world had waited expectantly for its launching and again for its sailing; had read accounts of its tremendous size and its unexampled completeness and luxury; had felt it a matter of the greatest satisfaction that such a comfortable, and above all such a safe boat had been designed and built—the "unsinkable lifeboat";—and then in a moment to hear that it had gone to the bottom as if it had been the veriest tramp steamer of a few hundred tons; and with it fifteen hundred passengers, some of them known the world over! The improbability of such a thing ever happening was what staggered humanity.*

Just three days after the Titanic disaster, a news article showed that the captain himself wholeheartedly believed the Titanic to be unsinkable.

Captain Believed Titanic Was Unsinkable

(Erie, PA, April 17, 1912) That Captain Smith believed the Titanic and the Olympic to be absolutely unsinkable is recalled by a man who had a conversation with the veteran commander on a recent voyage of the Olympic.

The talk was concerning the accident in which the British warship Hawke rammed the Olympic.

"The commander of the Hawke was entirely to blame," commented a young officer who was in the group. "He was 'showing off' his war ship before a throng of passengers and made a miscalculation."

---

* Lawrence Beesley, *The Loss of the S.S. Titanic: Its Story and Its Lessons* (Boston and New York: Houghton Mifflin Company, 1912). <http://www.titanic-titanic.com/loss_of_the_ss_titanic_1.shtml> (7 June 2004)

Captain Smith smiled enigmatically at the theory advanced by his subordinate, but made no comment as to this view of the mishap.

"Anyhow," declared Captain Smith, "the Olympic is unsinkable, and Titanic will be the same when she is put in commission.

"Why," he continued, "either of these vessels could be cut in halves and each half would remain afloat almost indefinitely. The non-sinkable vessel has been reached in these two wonderful craft.

"I venture to add," concluded Captain Smith, "that even if the engines and boilers of these vessels were to fall through their bottoms, the vessels would remain afloat."*

Even after the ship hit the iceberg, before news spread of just how deadly the accident had been, White Star Line vice president Phillip Franklin over optimistically reassured newspapers that everything was fine. "There is no danger that Titanic will sink," he was quoted as saying. "The boat is unsinkable and nothing but inconvenience will be suffered by the passengers."†

Do you see how confident everyone was in the Titanic before its tragic end? Until the Titanic went down, everyone sincerely believed it was unsinkable. When faced with the facts of a sinking ship, however, such sincerity wasn't worth a dime. All the faith in the world couldn't stop that boat from going down.

---

* <http://ourworld.compuserve.com/homepages/Carpathia/page2.htm> (8 June 2004)

† <http://www.webtitanic.net/framequotes.html> (8 June 2004)

Remember, faith is only as good as the object upon which it is placed. Passengers, captains, crew members, family members—practically everyone had firm faith in the unsinkability of the Titanic. But as this example from history so poignantly shows, *firm* faith does not equal *good* faith. Faith is only good when its object is good.

How many people today are placing their faith in Titanics? There are thousands of different religions and world-views on this planet, many of them claiming completely opposite "truths." Sure, all these people may be "sincere" in their beliefs, just as many were sincere in believing the Titanic could not be sunk. But some of them are also sincerely wrong, for all these "truths" cannot coexist. There is no way that *all* these "truths" can be right, just as there was no way the Titanic was both sinkable *and* unsinkable. One or the other has to be true.

> Firm faith does not equal good faith.

While sincerity might be admirable, it simply is not good enough in and of itself when it comes to faith. The sincerest person in the world could be dead wrong in his or her beliefs, and that sincerity won't help one iota in making his or her beliefs right. Truth is truth, whether you sincerely believe in it or not.

DAY THREE

Our Christian faith is valuable because its object is priceless.

So, you might be asking, what about the Christian faith? If faith is only as good as its object, how good is the Christian faith?

My friends, I can give this answer to you with 100 percent certainty, a lifetime warranty (make that an "eternal" lifetime warranty), and a money-back guarantee:

The Christian faith is VERY GOOD! Why do I say this with such certainty? Because the object of the Christian faith is very good, as well.

The object I'm talking about is not some mere mortal or a created fictitious god or an undefined spiritual force or anything of the sort. This "object" is none other than Jesus Christ Himself. God incarnate, "in the flesh." Emmanuel, or "God with us"!

Christ Jesus,...being in the form of God, did not consider it robbery to be equal with God, but made Himself of no

reputation, taking the form of a bondservant, and coming in the likeness of men. And being found in appearance as a man, He humbled Himself and became obedient to the point of death, even the death of the cross. Therefore God also has highly exalted Him and given Him the name which is above every name, that at the name of Jesus every knee should bow, of those in heaven, and of those on earth, and of those under the earth, and that every tongue should confess that Jesus Christ is Lord, to the glory of God the Father. (Philippians 2:5–11)

As these verses from Philippians tell us, the object of our faith, the One in whom we place our trust, came and lived among us. Not only that, He died for us while He was here— and then rose from the grave to conquer death and sin forever! This truly is amazing grace.

Unfortunately, though, not everybody sees this. The time has not yet come for *"every knee* [to] *bow"* and *"every tongue* [to] *confess"* the lordship of Jesus Christ. Many scoff at Christianity today, believing that it's the Titanic all over again. They believe we, as Christians, have based our faith in a fairy tale, that we're going to be sadly disappointed someday when we see they were right all along.

Again, I can say with all confidence that Christians are not putting their faith in a ship that's going to sink. In reality, it's the world around us that's heading full-speed, on an already sinking ship, for an immovable iceberg up ahead. And we were on that same crash course ourselves before putting faith in Jesus Christ! By His grace, however, we are now safe and secure.

For those who doubt the truthfulness of Christianity, they are welcome to do research of their own. For the sake of space, by no means can I include an apologetic of the Christian faith

here. Suffice it to say, though, there is a ton of proof out there. If someone you know, or even you yourself, has doubts about the Christian faith, look into those doubts! Trust me; the Christian faith can handle it.

Believe it or not, several great men of faith in the history of the church came to faith because they were skeptics first who sought to prove Christianity wrong. When they embarked on their academic quests, however, all evidence pointed to the absolute certainty and indisputable truthfulness of Christianity.

> Our Christian faith is not a sinking ship.

C. S. Lewis, for example, the great Christian author of *Mere Christianity, The Problem of Pain, The Chronicles of Narnia*, and other great books, went through a path of deep skepticism and atheism before becoming a Christian.

Christian author Josh MacDowell was also a skeptic and atheist for many years; when he began researching history to debunk the Christian "myth," however, he found himself face-to-face with evidence he couldn't dispute. The apologetic book *Evidence That Demands a Verdict* shares that evidence with interested readers.

Don't take my word for it. I encourage you to do the research. When all is said and done, I think you'll find the Christian faith to be solid, trustworthy, and reliable. Praise God for the invaluable faith He has given us!

Day Four

Christian faith goes beyond mere belief in God.

Only 3 percent of Americans believe there is no such thing as God according to a 2004 poll by George Barna.[*] Sounds pretty promising, doesn't it? If only 3 percent don't believe in a God, that must mean 97 percent of Americans believe in God. That's great news, isn't it?!

Well, if those 97 percent of Americans believed in the great I Am as presented in the Bible, then perhaps this would be good news. Unfortunately, just because someone says he "believes in God" doesn't mean he's spiritually on track.

Here's a more detailed breakdown of that 97 percent who "believe in God."

- 4 percent believe everyone is God.

- 69 percent believe that God is the all-powerful, all-knowing, perfect Creator who rules the world today.

---

[*] <http://www.barna.org/FlexPage.aspx?Page=Topic&TopicID=5> (8 June 2004)

- 7 percent believe that God is the total realization of personal, human potential.

- 4 percent believe that there are many gods, each with different power and authority.

- 9 percent believe that God is a state of higher consciousness that a person may reach.*

So, out of that 97 percent of "believers," some believe that *we are* gods, some think we can *become* gods, some think there are *many* gods, and some think "god" is just an *expression* for mankind reaching its full potential. This doesn't sound like good news to me.

Fortunately, according to the statistic, the majority of Americans (69 percent) do believe that "God is the all-powerful, all-knowing, perfect creator who rules the world today." But even many of these "believers" might be bowing down to a different god than the God of the Bible.

> A person can believe yet still be faithless.

Or perhaps they're not even bowing down at all.

You see, mere *belief* is not *faith*. Even when a man believes in the right God, he might still be "faithless." A man or woman can believe that the true God, the God of the Bible, exists until he or she is blue in the face. Until that *belief* leads to *obedience* and *trust,* however, it is far from biblical *faith.*

The Bible drives this point home in the New Testament book of James. James wrote,

> *You believe that there is one God. You do well. Even the demons believe; and tremble!* (James 2:19)

---

* <http://www.barna.org/FlexPage.aspx?Page=Topic&TopicID=5> (8 June 2004)

James reminded us that even demons believe there is a God. Come to think of it, wouldn't it be pretty strange if demons *didn't* believe in God? Most Christians agree that Satan and his demons are fallen angels—angels who used to reside in heaven, in God's very presence. It would be quite odd for them *not* to believe in God. They've seen Him face-to-face—they know He exists! You'll never hear a demon question the existence of God. They *know* He's real.

But just because demons acknowledge God's existence, do we say that they have faith in Him? Of course not! They *believe* there is a God, but they do not put *faith* in Him. They are faithless rebels against God, complete renegades.

And so are we—until we exercise faith in God by accepting His gift of salvation.

Do you believe in God? Good. That's a start. But how is your faith? Are you content to stay in the realm of belief, simply acknowledging that there is a God? Or have you moved beyond belief into the realm of faith—the realm where we bow down before God, acknowledging not just that He exists but that He is Ruler, Maker, and Redeemer of all?

It's my prayer that you're living in faith. *You* might be content to stay in the realm of mere belief, but *God* is not content for you to do so. He's ready for you to walk in faith, acknowledging His sovereignty through absolute obedience, trust, and worship in all that you do.

DAY FIVE

True faith means accepting God as God.

I n the last chapter I asked the question, Do you believe in God? Now, my guess is that, since you're reading this book about Christian faith, you probably believe in God, specifically, the three-in-one God—Father, Son, and Holy Spirit—as presented in the Bible. If I'm wrong in this assumption, please forgive me. (But I do encourage you to keep reading nonetheless!)

For those of you who answer, "Yes, I believe in the God of the Bible," let me take it a step further: Do you believe that God is God? No, that's not a typo. You read it right the first time: Do you believe that God is God?

You see, just as there's a difference between *believing in God* and *having faith in God*, there's a vast difference between simply *believing in God* and *believing that God is God.* Let me explain.

As we saw in the last chapter, believing in God—at its most basic level—means simply acknowledging the existence of God. So when someone says, "I believe in God," all we can really

gather from that statement is that he or she believes God exists. Being able to say, "I believe that God is God," however, takes that simple belief to a whole new level. This is where faith starts to kick in. This is where a person moves beyond just saying, "Yes, I believe God exists" to "Yes, I accept His sovereignty, or His 'God-ship,' over my life."

True faith requires us to accept and acknowledge God as the Ruler and Sovereign that He is.

Have you ever stopped to think about the many names God has throughout the Scriptures? In Old Testament times, names meant a lot, for they were often used to express a person's character, the circumstances of his or her birth, or even that person's destiny. Jacob and Esau are a perfect example. We find the account of their birth and naming in Genesis 25:24–26.

> True faith accepts God's "God-ship."

So when [Rebekah's] days were fulfilled for her to give birth, indeed there were twins in her womb. And the first came out red. He was like a hairy garment all over; so they called his name Esau. Afterward his brother came out, and his hand took hold of Esau's heel; so his name was called Jacob.

In the original Hebrew, *Esau* means "hairy," and *Jacob* means "supplanter." These names were perfect for this set of twins! Esau was definitely hairy, and starting from the very moment of birth, Jacob was continually trying to "supplant" his brother's firstborn status—a goal he finally accomplished by duping Esau into selling his birthright and tricking Isaac into giving him Esau's blessing.

Well, just as people's names were significant in Old Testament times, God's names are significant, too, for they express attributes of His very character and nature. Many of

these names focus on the sovereignty of God—in other words, His God-ship. Essentially, these names proclaim loud and clear, "This God is the true God—and He is truly God!" For example, in the Old Testament, the Hebrew words *El, Yahweh,* and *Adonai* are frequently used when referring to God, and each one emphasizes something slightly different about God's character. *El* focuses on God's strength. *Yahweh* emphasizes God's self-existent nature. And *Adonai* emphasizes God's authority.

All of these names, and the many more used throughout Scripture, remind us of our Lord's "God-ness"—His supreme sovereignty and rulership over all creation. What a mighty God He is! He is God, period. As such, we had better be ready to accept anything and everything that comes from His hand. As Oswald Chambers wrote,

> Faith for my deliverance is not faith in God. Faith means, whether I am visibly delivered or not, I will stick to my belief that God is love. There are some things only learned in a fiery furnace.*

True faith accepts the God-ship of God, no questions asked.

True faith says, "God, if You want to destroy the whole world right now, I won't complain. You made it, so You're certainly allowed to unmake it whenever You want."

True faith embraces everything that comes from God's hand, no matter how difficult or confusing those things may be.

True faith realizes that God, as Creator, Ruler, and Sustainer of all, is "allowed" to do whatever He pleases whenever He pleases to do it.

---

* Oswald Chambers, *Run Today's Race.* <http://www.christianglobe. com/Illustrations/theDetails.asp?whichOne=h&whichFile=healing> (7 June 2004)

True faith does not complain, for it knows that God is the Standard and Standard-Maker.

True faith accepts that God, and God alone, is in charge of all things.

True faith says, "My God, You are God. There is no one greater than You."

Are you walking in true faith? Have you come to the point of accepting God's "God-ship"? Or are you still questioning His sovereignty, His power, His might, His control? Wherever you are, I challenge you to take a moment to reflect on the awesomeness of God. Realize that He is your Maker, you are His creation, and He is the One who's in charge. Teach your heart to say with certainty, "God, You are God."

Day Six

Faith means believing God is good.

Fortunately for us, God's "God-ness" does not exclude His goodness. In fact, His goodness is part and parcel of His "God-ness." When we understand God by faith, we come to realize that He is wholly and completely good. In fact, His very nature defines goodness.

> *Oh, taste and see that the Lord is good; blessed is the man who trusts in Him!* (Psalm 34:8)

> *For the Lord is good; His mercy is everlasting, and His truth endures to all generations.* (Psalm 100:5)

> *Praise the Lord, for the Lord is good; sing praises to His name, for it is pleasant.* (Psalm 135:3)

> *The Lord is good to all, and His tender mercies are over all His works.* (Psalm 145:9)

> *The Lord is good to those who wait for Him, to the soul who seeks Him.* (Lamentations 3:25)

> *The Lord is good, a stronghold in the day of trouble; and He knows those who trust in Him.* (Nahum 1:7)

Do you get the picture? Our God is a good God! So many people have this horrible image in their heads when they think of God. They envision some mean, despotic, power-hungry ruler who wants nothing more than to punish them on the spot, even strike them dead if needed. In their minds, God is just waiting for them to slip up. He likes it when they sin because then He has an excuse to bring them punishment and pain.

Nothing could be further from the truth. As we see from verses such as the ones listed above, our God is anything but cruel and heartless. He is good, merciful, and loving.

For You, Lord, are good, and ready to forgive, and abundant in mercy to all those who call upon You. (Psalm 86:5)

Starting to get the picture? Now don't misunderstand. Some people go too far with the "God is love" message to the point of forgetting that He is just, too. He has high standards of righteousness, standards that we—as fallen human beings—come short of. Our falling short grieves Him, and He cannot just overlook our sins. That would fly in the face of His justness, His righteousness. What He did do, however, was provide His Son as the perfect, pure, and spotless sacrifice. This was the greatest expression of love, and it was this gift that allowed God to forgive us completely without contradicting His just and righteous nature.

For God so loved the world that He gave His only begotten Son, that whoever believes in Him should not perish but have everlasting life. (John 3:16)

But God demonstrates His own love toward us, in that while we were still sinners, Christ died for us.

(Romans 5:8)

Let me give you a little example that helps clarify God's simultaneous "goodness" and "God-ness." As usual, the things

of earth are but shadows of the things of heaven. This example won't even come close to expressing the glorious mysteries of God—but it'll help a little.

Imagine a potter, an expert potter at that. We'll call him Theo. Now Theo is a true artist, renowned the world over. He's had hundreds of exhibitions, and it's not uncommon for one of his pieces to fetch upwards of a thousand dollars. Devotees recognize his work by his trademark signature—an impression of his own thumb on the bottom of each piece. He's well-known among artists and considered to be the best of the best by those who know pottery. In short, Theo is good. Very good. When it comes to pottery, he knows his stuff.

> God's goodness is part and parcel of His Godness.

Now go with me in your mind's eye for just a minute to Theo's studio. He's at the potter's wheel, working away. Already several completed pieces line the countertop in his studio, pieces he had been working on for months. Each one has been stamped with the signature thumbprint, and they sit there patiently, just waiting to be shipped off to the next exhibition. As perfect works of art, they are a testament to the expert mastery of their creator.

Now imagine that, through no fault of Theo's, one of those pieces were to fall off the countertop. Perhaps someone slammed a door down the hall, and it shook the countertop enough to knock one of those works of pottery straight down to the ground. You know the outcome: hundreds of little pottery pieces everywhere. Shards and shards and shards with no end. The piece is so obliterated that even Theo's signature thumbprint cannot be discerned.

Perhaps you've figured out my little illustration already. "Theo" is like our Lord, the Creator God who lovingly and expertly

crafted each one of us. We are His works of art. And just like Theo's pieces of pottery, we have been "printed" with not just a thumbprint, but with the very image of God!

> *Then God said, "Let Us make man in Our image, accord-ing to Our likeness; let them have dominion over the fish of the sea, over the birds of the air, and over the cattle, over all the earth and over every creeping thing that creeps on the earth." So God created man in His own image; in the image of God He created him; male and female He created them.* (Genesis 1:26–27)

Just as Theo's piece of pottery fell, so too have we fallen. When Adam and Eve sinned in the garden, they fell from the heights God had placed them in. They also marred the "image of God" that had been placed in them, just as the thumbprint was destroyed in the fallen piece of clay.

Now, as I said before, the analogy isn't perfect. One major difference is that Theo's pottery wasn't at fault for its fall. It didn't suddenly grow legs and decide to jump off the countertop. Adam and Eve, however, knew what they were doing when they sinned. They willfully chose to make that sinful leap in defiance of God—and their offspring have been willfully choosing ever since that day.

That's another difference. The clay pot's action affected only itself. Adam and Eve's decision, however, has had ramifications all throughout history. We are still born into the sin they introduced.

But back to the illustration. Theo, when he sees the fallen pot, is obviously saddened. Every piece he makes is valuable in his eyes, and it pains him to see one of his works smashed and destroyed beyond recognition. But what's lost is lost, so he might as well grab a trash bin and start cleaning up, right?

Any lesser potter might have taken this route, but Theo is no ordinary potter. Yes, this piece of clay has been destroyed beyond recognition, but Theo still has plans for it. Plans to bring it back. And so he abandons his work at the potter's wheel and sets to lovingly gathering every tiny little piece of the shattered pot. When the fragments are all accounted for, he sets to carefully piecing and the pot back together, securing each piece together with fresh new clay from his potter's wheel.

This, my friends, is similar to the work God does in our lives. He is a righteous God, a God who would have been completely justified in leaving us helpless in our wicked ways—or even just flat-out destroying us! No one would have batted an eye if Theo had chosen to throw his broken pot away; as creator of the pot, he would have been justified in doing so. How much more justified would the Creator of all have been in abandoning or destroying the creatures who had rebelled against Him?

As a good God, however, He chose to redeem us, to provide a way for us to return back to how we were meant to be. Just as Theo the patient potter carefully pieced the broken jar back together, our Lord lovingly renews and revives our sinful, broken lives. For Theo, all it took was some time and extra clay. For our righteous Lord, however, it took the death and resurrection of His very own Son. Talk about paying a high price!

I hope this little illustration, feeble though it may be, has helped you to better understand how good our God really is. Have you experienced that goodness for yourself? Have you yet *"taste*[d] *and see*[n] *that the LORD is good"* (Psalm 34:8)? In response to His goodness, have you put your trust in Him? It is my prayer that, as you grow in faith, you will come to a deeper recognition and appreciation for the wonderful goodness and graciousness of our merciful, loving Lord.

DAY SEVEN

Faith is not a feeling.

Feelings come and feelings go
And feelings are deceiving;
My warrant is the Word of God,
Naught else is worth believing.
—Martin Luther*

When many people hear the word *faith,* they think it's something you feel. When you ask them why they believe what they believe, they'll say something like, "Well, I just *feel* that this is right. My heart tells me it is true."

You'd be surprised how many people confuse faith with feelings, even in the church. "As soon as I believed," they'll say, "this overwhelming sense of peace came over me." Now don't get me wrong. The Bible does assure us that there is a peace of God that *"surpasses all understanding"* (Philippians 4:7), and emotions are wonderful things, true

---

* <http://www.christianglobe.com/Illustrations/theDetails.asp?which One=f&whichFile=feelings> (7 June 2004)

gifts from God. He has made us to be creatures of emotion, people of feeling. We must not, however, rely *solely* upon our feelings and emotions.

You see, when Adam and Eve fell in the garden, their emotions fell, too. Ever since that day, mankind's emotions have been fickle, misleading, and often plain wrong! You know what I'm talking about. One minute you'll feel happy, the next minute sad; one minute calm, the next minute enraged. There's never any telling how we're going to feel from one minute to the next, or if what we're feeling actually makes sense with what's going on around us.

Can you imagine a world in which all of our decisions were based on our feelings? Children wouldn't be the only ones wanting ice cream for breakfast, lunch, and dinner—parents would, too! Except for the fortunate few who actually live, love, and breathe their jobs, no one would ever put in a full day's work—that's *if* they even chose to work at all. And as for friendships—we'd be lucky if those still existed since we'd probably be ruining them left and right by verbalizing whatever we felt, regardless of the feelings of those around us. An existence led by emotions would, in a word, be chaos.

> When Adam and Eve fell, their emotions fell, too.

Because of this, we cannot base our actions and decisions solely upon our feelings, no matter how noble those feelings may seem to be at the time. Instead, we must live by faith, and faith is far more than feelings. Faith is belief—founded in fact, emboldened by the Spirit, and shown through action. Faith is something we *live out* through our choices and decisions.

J. Allan Petersen tells a story in his book *The Myth of the Greener Grass* about a columnist and pastor named Dr. George

Crane. According to the story, a woman came into Dr. Crane's office full of extreme anger toward her husband. "I don't just want to leave him," she essentially said. "I want to hurt him. I want to hurt him as much as he's hurt me, and *then* divorce him."

Dr. Crane's response was unique. "Go home and *act* like you love your husband," he said. "Be as kind, giving, complimentary, and polite as possible. Go out of your way to make him feel special, appreciated, loved, and important. Convince him that you actually love him. After you've done all this, it will *really* hurt when you tell him you're leaving." "Great idea!" she said, and she eagerly went home to put her plan into action.

When she didn't return, Dr. Crane decided to give her a call. "Are you ready for that divorce now?" he asked her. "Divorce?!" she said. "Are you kidding? I've realized that I really do love him—and he's become a different man."*

As this example shows, our behavior can determine our feelings. This woman's actions completely transformed the frustration and anger she had toward her husband into loving tenderness. Motion resulted in emotion.

Frequently faith works much the same way. There will be many times in your life as a Christian when you'll have to do things you don't necessarily *feel* like doing. Maybe it's telling that hard-to-talk-to relative about Christ. Perhaps it's holding your tongue when you're itching to say some not-so-wholesome words. Or maybe it's just rolling out of bed early to spend time with God when your flesh is screaming, "Press the snooze button! Press the snooze button!"

---

* Story retold from J. Allan Petersen's *The Myth of the Greener Grass* (Carol Stream, Ill.: Tyndale, 1992).

The good news is that the more we walk in faith, the more our feelings start lining up with that faith. The more often you take steps of faith by sharing Christ with those hard-to-talk-to relatives, the more you will probably start enjoying these witnessing opportunities. The more you bite your lip when foul words are trying to get out, the more you'll desire to remove those words from your vocabulary entirely. And the more you resist the urge to reset your alarm in the morning, the easier it will be to rise for those early morning devotions. You see, faith doesn't always walk in step with our feelings.

Day Eight

Faith demands action.

We're all familiar with the stock Hollywood phrase "Lights! Camera! Action!" Well, it's my opinion that the "*Holy*-wood" version—the version that applies to our Christian walks—should go something like this: "Life! Faith! Action!"

Why? you ask. Good question. As always, God's Word says it better than we, as mere humans, could ever hope to, so let's turn there first.

Almost the entire book of James deals with the issue of works and how good works—or "Action!"—relate to our faith. We'll focus on the last half of James 2, which really zeros in on this issue of faith in action. James wrote,

> *What does it profit, my brethren, if someone says he has faith but does not have works? Can faith save him? If a brother or sister is naked and destitute of daily food, and one of you says to them, "Depart in peace, be warmed and filled," but you do not give them the things which are needed for the body, what does it*

profit? ***Thus also faith by itself, if it does not have works, is dead.*** *But someone will say, "You have faith, and I have works." Show me your faith without your works, and* ***I will show you my faith by my works.***
(James 2:14–18, emphasis added)

Back in the early church, there were some people in the church teaching a very dangerous message, a message that sometimes still creeps into our church walls—in disguise, of course. This dangerous message was called "antinomianism," which was just a fancy way of saying "against the law." In other words, people who buy into antinomianism think that, since we are saved by God's grace—apart from works and not by the Law—we are now free from even having to obey the Law. Such people basically say, "Since we're free from the penalty of the Law, and since we're saved by grace through faith, let's sin up a storm! It's all forgiven, so why not?"

James, however, reminded his readers—as well as us today—that such an attitude is exactly *opposite* of the one we should have as Christians. While it's true that we're not saved *by* our works, that doesn't mean works aren't important. In fact, they are *extremely* important, for they're nothing more than our faith in action. *"Show me your faith without your works, and I will show you my faith by my works"* (James 2:18).

So, back to our little "Holy-wood" expression. "Life! Faith! Action!" Are you starting to see the progression? First, we are given a new life. Before we can walk in true faith and show that faith through good works, we have to be redeemed. Without Jesus as our Lord first, we won't have a clue about how to walk in faith! We must receive the new life that comes only through Jesus Christ. This is the "Life!" part of the process.

Day Eight

After our new life comes growth in faith. As we daily commune with our new Lord and Savior, we find our faith increasing and being strengthened, day by day. This is the "Faith!" part of the process.

Part of the way we show this growth in faith is through our actions and deeds. As we daily spend time with the Lord in our new "Life!" and as we consequently begin to grow in "Faith!" good works will follow. This is the "Action!" part of the process.

> We're not saved by works, but works are still important.

Notice that none of these things is independent of the other. Just as you can't have "Action!" in Hollywood without the "Lights!" and the "Camera!" you can't have truly good deeds, or actions, without new life in Christ and the faith that accompanies it. New life, faith, and action are all interrelated. They need each other to survive.

If you're not adding action to your faith, you're not really living out your calling as a child of God. As Christians,

> *We are His workmanship, created in Christ Jesus for good works, which God prepared beforehand that we should walk in them.* (Ephesians 2:10)

Earlier in his epistle, James had another important message concerning works. He made a point of reminding his readers that if they only *hear* the Word of God but do not *do* what it says, they're only fooling themselves. True faith will always show itself through action:

> *But be doers of the word, and not hearers only, deceiving yourselves. For if anyone is a hearer of the word and not a doer, he is like a man observing his natural*

face in a mirror; for he observes himself, goes away, and immediately forgets what kind of man he was. But he who looks into the perfect law of liberty and continues in it, and is not a forgetful hearer but a doer of the work, this one will be blessed in what he does.

(James 1:22–25)

How's your faith walk? Is your faith showing itself through action? Remember,

He who says he abides in Him ought himself also to walk just as He walked. (1 John 2:6)

Day Nine

Faith demands knowledge.

In the modern church, it's a sad but true fact that many are abandoning serious study of God's Word. Not wanting to seem "too intellectual" for fear that will make them seem out of touch with the Spirit, they end up essentially throwing away their Bibles altogether. They hardly ever crack the cover of God's Word, let alone spend some serious time meditating on it.

Let me tell you something, folks. God's Word is His standard for our lives. We can't afford *not* to study Scripture. If we want to know who God is and how He works, we've got to open the Book! We need biblical knowledge. Period.

Second Timothy 2:15 couldn't make this point any clearer. It says,

> *Be diligent* ["*study*" KJV] *to present yourself approved to God, a worker who does not need to be ashamed, rightly dividing the word of truth.*

If someone had any doubts about whether or not they should be studying and building up their knowledge base,

this verse shoots those doubts down in a heartbeat. As Christians, part of our calling is to be "students" of God's Word.

On the other end of the spectrum are those people who desperately want knowledge but are looking in all the wrong places for it. "There's nothing worthwhile in that old, dusty book," they say. "How can studying a book as ancient and outdated as the Bible help us grow in knowledge?"

I'll tell you how. The fact of the matter is that the Bible is *the* best place to go for knowledge because the information in its pages is *God-inspired,* not man-inspired. I don't know about you, but I'll take something from the hands of God over something from the hands of men any day! And as for outdated? I don't think so. The same God who created the world in Genesis, made the walls fall in Joshua, provided a Savior in the Gospels, and sent the Holy Spirit in Acts is the same God who's on the throne today.

Don't throw away your mind!

But back to the issue of those in the church who are afraid of seeming "too intellectual." Don't you know that the Holy Spirit will always be acting in accordance with God's Word? Just because you're a scholar of the Bible doesn't mean your heart has to be hardened to the Spirit's moving. You can be a serious Bible student while still walking in the Spirit. A strong heart and a strong mind are not mutually exclusive.

Remember what Jesus said to the woman at the well? He said,

But the hour is coming, and now is, when the true worshipers will worship the Father in spirit and truth; for

the Father is seeking such to worship Him. God is Spirit, and those who worship Him must worship in spirit and truth. (John 4:23–24)

Yes, *"true worshipers"* worship in Spirit. You've got that part of the equation right, my friends. But they also worship in truth. And how do we worship in truth? By first *knowing,* or *having knowledge of,* the truth—which means we need to start studying!

Please, my friends, don't throw your mind away. And by all means, don't throw your Bible away, either. Your mind is a gift, and God's Word is an even greater one. If you want to stay sensitive to the moving of the Spirit, then by all means work on building up your biblical knowledge. As you do so, you'll find your heart becoming even more sensitive to the Spirit, not less.

Increased knowledge does not mean decreased spiritual sensitivity. In fact, I'm sure the Spirit is saddened more than anything when He sees good-intentioned Christians neglect study in the name of fostering "heartfelt" worship. It is only once a person is able to *"rightly* [divide] *the word of truth"* (2 Timothy 2:15) that he or she can sincerely worship with a completely devoted heart.

Now understand, as with all things, there are extremes that should be avoided. The person who is so intent on gaining knowledge that he spends *all* his time memorizing genealogies and temple measurements is not being a true student of God's Word. Sure, you're welcome to memorize those things if you really want to, but you had better make sure you're also doing some study that leads to action.

Remember what James said—faith without action might as well be dead. If *all* your energies are going toward

memorizing facts and figures and *none* of your energies are going toward internalizing biblical knowledge and wisdom that will make your spirit grow, then quite frankly, you're wasting your time.

> *But be doers of the word, and not hearers only, deceiving yourselves. For if anyone is a hearer of the word and not a doer, he is like a man observing his natural face in a mirror; for he observes himself, goes away, and immediately forgets what kind of man he was. But he who looks into the perfect law of liberty and continues in it, and is not a forgetful hearer but a doer of the work, this one will be blessed in what he does.*
> (James 1:22–25)

True biblical knowledge walks hand in hand with the Spirit. It is my prayer that you will choose to be a serious student of God's Word, to grow in the knowledge God has ordained for you. As you do so, I guarantee you that your knowledge base will not "crowd out" your spiritual sensitivity. On the contrary, the Spirit will tap into the knowledge and make you more effective for the kingdom.

> *With my whole heart I have sought You; Oh, let me not wander from Your commandments! Your word I have hidden in my heart, that I might not sin against You! Blessed are You, O LORD! Teach me Your statutes!*
> (Psalm 119:10–12)

Praise God for the gifts of His Spirit and His Word!

Day Ten

Faith is our shield.

Let me ask you a few questions: Are you armored up? Are you ready for battle? Are you prepared to withstand attacks?

I certainly hope you are, because the fact of the matter is, we are at war. Yes, friends, we are at war. This is not physical warfare. No, this war is much more serious than that. This war has eternal consequences, for this war is spiritual.

> *For though we walk in the flesh, we do not war according to the flesh.* (2 Corinthians 10:3)

The fact of the matter is that, if you are a Christian, you are under attack. Satan and his forces do not want you praising God, and they'll go to any extreme to keep you from doing so. They want to distract you, turn your attention away from God, and keep you focused on anything but His kingdom. How do they do this? Through warfare.

> *Your adversary the devil walks about like a roaring lion, seeking whom he may devour.* (1 Peter 5:8)

Satan is on the prowl, and we'd be foolish to forget it. Unfortunately, though, this is how many Christians live— ignorant of the fact that they're at war. They fumble through life, forgetting that they've got an enemy out to get them. When temptations come, they're left scratching their heads, wondering, "Where did that come from?"

Can you imagine if soldiers in the physical realm behaved like that in battle? What if troops just went stumbling into enemy territory, never stopping to pull out their weapons and prepare for potential attack? That would be military suicide! But this is exactly what many Christians are doing.

Please understand, we don't lack supplies. As 2 Corinthians 10:4 reminds us, the weapons God has given us are more than up to the task.

For the weapons of our warfare are not carnal but mighty in God for pulling down strongholds.

Our Lord has equipped us for the battle—we just have to put that equipment to use!

Ephesians 6:10–17 is probably one of the most quoted passages when it comes to Scripture on spiritual warfare. In it, Paul showed us, in detail, the spiritual equipment that God has given us. Let's take a look:

Finally, my brethren, be strong in the Lord and in the power of His might. Put on the whole armor of God, that you may be able to stand against the wiles of the devil. For we do not wrestle against flesh and blood, but against principalities, against powers, against the rulers of the darkness of this age, against spiritual hosts of wickedness in the heavenly places. Therefore take up the whole armor of God, that you may be able to withstand in the evil day, and having done all, to

stand. Stand therefore, having girded your waist with truth, having put on the breastplate of righteousness, and having shod your feet with the preparation of the gospel of peace; above all, taking the shield of faith with which you will be able to quench all the fiery darts of the wicked one. And take the helmet of salvation, and the sword of the Spirit, which is the word of God.

Did you catch all that? We've got an entire set of armor prepared for us! A belt of truth, a breastplate of righteousness, a pair of gospel shoes, a shield of faith, a helmet of salvation, and a sword of the Spirit! We are definitely equipped and ready for battle. It's just a matter of putting that equipment on and actually using it!

> If you're a Christian, you're under attack.

Since this is a book on faith, I want to turn our attention specifically to the *"shield of faith."* Here's what Paul said about the *"shield of faith."*

Above all, taking the shield of faith with which you will be able to quench all the fiery darts of the wicked one. (Ephesians 6:16)

According to this verse, faith is one of the greatest weapons we have against temptation. It acts as a shield, keeping the *"fiery darts of the wicked one,"* or temptations, at bay. And not only does it turn the temptations away—it also quenches them!

I'd like to draw your attention to two little words in this verse that really that pack a punch. Notice that Paul wrote, *"Above all...."* Now, this could be interpreted several different ways. Matthew Henry, in his commentary, interpreted it to mean "most importantly." He wrote,

This is more necessary than any of them. Faith is all in all to us in an hour of temptation.*

In other words, faith is the most important piece of our spiritual armor. It is supreme.

The *"above all"* in this verse could also simply be reminding us of the versatility of faith. Just as a shield can be turned in any direction to protect from fiery darts, no matter where those fiery darts are coming from, our faith is able to quench temptation, no matter where it arises. Matthew Henry had something to say about this, too. He wrote,

The breast-plate [sic] secures the vitals; but with the shield we turn every way.†

The *Amplified Version* brings this meaning to light as well. It reads,

Lift up over all the [covering] shield of saving faith, upon which you can quench all the flaming missiles of the wicked [one]. (Ephesians 6:16 AMP)

Did you catch that? The shield covers all. It provides protection and safety, wherever that protection is needed. And our faith is just the same. Our God has equipped us with faith that can handle temptations in any shape or form. Praise God! Now let's put our shields to use!

---

* Matthew Henry, *Commentary on the Whole Bible* (1721), Vol. VI— Acts to Revelation, "Ephesians" (1721). <http://ccel.org/h/henry/mhc2/MHC49006.HTM> (7 June 2004)

† Ibid.

Day Eleven

Sometimes faith means giving up.

S ometimes faith means giving up. You heard me right; sometimes faith means giving up.

Now before you toss this book in the garbage and holler, "This guy's telling me to throw in the towel and give up!" hear me out. I'm not talking about throwing in the towel. I'm talking about giving up *all that's in your hands.* In other words, faith means *letting go* of everything that's keeping you from God.

Make more sense now?

We see this principle time and time again in Scripture. From Abraham to Zacchaeus, God repeatedly called the faithful and faithful wanna-bes to let go of what they had.

Take Abraham, for instance. God called this man of faith to leave behind his homeland:

Now the Lord had said to Abram: "Get out of your country, from your family and from your father's house, to a land that I will show you. *I will make you*

a great nation; I will bless you and make your name
great; and you shall be a blessing. I will bless those who
bless you, and I will curse him who curses you; and in
you all the families of the earth shall be blessed."

(Genesis 12:1–3, emphasis added)

Or consider Zacchaeus. Now, this man had a lot to give up because he was rich. Very rich. As head tax collector, he had a lot of money to his name—lots of other people's money to be precise. (It was standard for the tax collectors to make their wealth by overcharging their clients and then pocketing the profits for themselves.) Despite this great wealth, it seems that Zacchaeus knew something was missing in his life—something that only the Savior could fill:

> *Then Jesus entered and passed through Jericho. Now*
> *behold, there was a man named Zacchaeus who was*
> *a chief tax collector, and he was rich. And he sought*
> *to see who Jesus was, but could not because of the*
> *crowd, for he was of short stature. So he ran ahead*
> *and climbed up into a sycamore tree to see Him, for He*
> *was going to pass that way. And when Jesus came to*
> *the place, He looked up and saw him, and said to him,*
> *"Zacchaeus, make haste and come down, for today I*
> *must stay at your house." So he made haste and came*
> *down, and received Him joyfully.*   (Luke 19:1–6)

The townspeople were none too happy to see Jesus visiting with this man who had swindled them time and time again. "[Jesus] *has gone to be a guest with a man who is a sinner,"* they complained (verse 7). But Zacchaeus was getting ready to turn over a new leaf.

> *Then Zacchaeus stood and said to the Lord,* **"Look,**
> **Lord, I give half of my goods to the poor; and if I**

have taken anything from anyone by false accusation, I restore fourfold." And Jesus said to him, "Today salvation has come to this house, because he also is a son of Abraham; for the Son of Man has come to seek and to save that which was lost."

(verses 8–10, emphasis added)

You see, Zacchaeus was ready for a faith-filled life, a life that had Christ—not money—at its center. This tax collector so desperately wanted to be a man of faith that he repented of his underhanded business methods—even to the point of *giving up* a large chunk of change. Why? Because sometimes a life of faith means giving things up.

It could be anything—a bad relationship, money, your car, even your family!

If anyone comes to Me and does not hate his father and mother, wife and children, brothers and sisters, yes, and his own life also, he cannot be My disciple.

(Luke 14:26)

Jesus wasn't telling us to hate our families here. He was just showing, by exaggeration, how all other loves in our lives should be like hate when compared to the love we have for Jesus Christ. He is to come first and foremost, above all things.

Giving things up is not always easy. Do you remember the story of the rich man who asked Jesus how to get to heaven? The Bible says he was actually *"grieved"* when he found out Jesus wanted him to let go of his riches:

Now as [Jesus] was going out on the road, one came running, knelt before Him, and asked Him, "Good Teacher, what shall I do that I may inherit eternal life?" So Jesus said to him, "Why do you call Me good? No

one is good but One, that is, God. "You know the commandments: 'Do not commit adultery,' 'Do not murder,' 'Do not steal,' 'Do not bear false witness,' 'Do not defraud,' 'Honor your father and your mother.'" And he answered and said to Him, "Teacher, all these things I have kept from my youth." Then Jesus, looking at him, loved him, and said to him, "One thing you lack: Go your way, sell whatever you have and give to the poor, and you will have treasure in heaven; and come, take up the cross, and follow Me." But he was sad at this word, and went away sorrowful, for he had great possessions. Then Jesus looked around and said to His disciples, "How hard it is for those who have riches to enter the kingdom of God!" And the disciples were astonished at His words. But Jesus answered again and said to them, "Children, how hard it is for those who trust in riches to enter the kingdom of God! It is easier for a camel to go through the eye of a needle than for a rich man to enter the kingdom of God."

(Mark 10:17–25)

This man was eager to please the *"Good Master."* As soon as he realized the cost, though, he bolted. His possessions were too near to his heart, and he would not give them up. What a horrible choice this man made! The Son of God is so much greater than these material goods! Despite his foolish choice, though, it's probably better that he left Jesus then and there instead of trying to "eat his cake and have it too," so to speak.

What is God telling you to "give up"?

Can you imagine if he had refused to sell his possessions as Christ had commanded him, but he still tried to follow after the Lord? He would have been lugging his trunkfuls of wealth all over the Judean countryside. While

Christ would have been trying to spread the kingdom of God, this man would have been close behind, unintentionally spreading his kingdom of avarice and greed. Do you think Christ would have put up with that for very long? I don't think so!

> *So then, because you are lukewarm, and neither cold
> nor hot, I will vomit you out of My mouth.*
>
> (Revelation 3:16)

If he'd tried to follow Christ AND keep the things that Christ was telling him to give up, I'm sure he would have been reprimanded and rebuked. But how many of us in the church are doing essentially the same thing? How many of us have heard Christ say, "You must give _____ up if you are going to follow Me in faith," but then we turn around and carry that thing through the desert, our own "trunkload" that we can't seem to surrender.

God's Word is clear: When He calls us to give things up, we better give them up. If we don't, we're walking in wishy-washy, lukewarm faith.

DAY TWELVE

Faith must be fueled by love.

Almost all of us have heard the expression "love makes the world go 'round." Most people think of romantic love when they hear the phrase, but if we were to think of the saying in terms of agape love, or Christlike love, then there's actually a hint of biblical truth in this frequently used secular expression.

We've spent a lot of time so far talking about faith—which is appropriate, I suppose, since this is a book entitled *40 Days to Faith*! I hope you've come to a deeper understanding as you've read this book of how critical it is to have faith—solid, biblical, Christian faith, that is. All that being said, however, faith won't make a bit of difference if it's not accompanied by love. As Paul put it, you can have faith enough to move entire mountains, but without love, you've got nothing!

> *Though I speak with the tongues of men and of angels, but have not love, I have become sounding brass or a clanging cymbal. And though I have the gift of prophecy,*

and understand all mysteries and all knowledge, **and though I have all faith, so that I could remove mountains, but have not love, I am nothing.** *And though I bestow all my goods to feed the poor, and though I give my body to be burned, but have not love, it profits me nothing.* (1 Corinthians 13:1–3, emphasis added)

Through Paul, the Holy Spirit made a big statement here. "If you don't have love," the Spirit basically said, "your good works, your spiritual gifts, and even your faith itself aren't worth a dime."

Some of you might get defensive at this point and argue back. "But I know how to speak in tongues!" you might say, or, "Have you heard me use my gift of prophecy?" Perhaps you'd remind the Lord of your great faith—faith big enough to move mountains! Or maybe you'd refresh His memory about your willingness to go anywhere for Him—even to the point of martyrdom!

You know what the Holy Spirit would say back to you at this point? Probably the same thing Christ said to Peter three times in John 21: *"Do you love Me?"* (verses 15–17). This is what is most important in God's eyes: our love for Him. And if we do profess love for Him, then we better be ready to put that love in action. As Jesus said to Peter in that same passage, *"Feed My sheep."* If we love Him, we must show it through love to others. Scripture repeats this message over and over again.

[Jesus said,] *"By this all will know that you are My disciples, if you have love for one another."* (John 13:35)

And this is His commandment: that we should believe on the name of His Son Jesus Christ and love one another, as He gave us commandment. Now he who

keeps His commandments abides in Him, and He in him. And by this we know that He abides in us, by the Spirit whom He has given us. (1 John 3:23–24)

Beloved, let us love one another, for love is of God; and everyone who loves is born of God and knows God. He who does not love does not know God, for God is love. In this the love of God was manifested toward us, that God has sent His only begotten Son into the world, that we might live through Him. In this is love, not that we loved God, but that He loved us and sent His Son to be the propitiation for our sins. Beloved, if God so loved us, we also ought to love one another....No one has seen God at any time. If we love one another, God abides in us, and His love has been perfected in us. By this we know that we abide in Him, and He in us, because He has given us of His Spirit. (1 John 4:7–13)

If you want to know how to love, you don't have to look any farther than your Bible. In its pages, you'll find the ultimate example of love: sacrificing a Son—an only Son—to redeem fallen humanity.

So many times people think love is something you just feel, an emotion and nothing more. Nothing could be further from the truth. Don't think that God sent His Son to earth just because He "felt" like it, or that Jesus gave up His life on the cross simply because His emotions were pulling Him in that direction. I don't think so! God sent His Son to die a cruel death on a cross because He chose to love His redeemed—not because he felt like it.

> Faith without love is nothing.

The same holds true for us. We may not "feel" like doing the loving thing in a situation, but if we desire to please

God, then we will choose to love with agape love. And how do we display that love? We show it through our actions, because agape love is a love of action.

A little more than ten years ago, a Pentecostal church in southern Florida asked me to help conduct a healing crusade. They'd heard about the miracles God had been doing through my ministry in other parts of the south and, believing it was God's timing, they invited me to come lead a crusade in their own small town.

Before the first crusade meeting began, the members of the church said they were praying for a great move of God. I stood in total agreement with them. To my delight, many people from the community flocked to the meetings, where they received miraculous healings and, more importantly, salvation of their souls as they surrendered their lives to Christ. Our prayers were being answered!

Not everyone in the church, however, felt the same way. Many of the new converts were black, which made some members of this primarily white church uncomfortable.

About halfway through the week, the head deacon of the church, who was also the chairman of the trustee board, confronted the pastor. He voiced his strong (and wrong!) opinion that there were too many black people coming to the meetings, which could be detrimental to the image of the church.

Fortunately the head pastor stuck it out. It would have been easy for him to capitulate and concede to the angry deacon, especially a deacon with so much influence! The pastor knew, however, that the church was doing God's work. To have stopped reaching out to people at that time would have been to slow down the work of the kingdom. The pastor frankly told the head deacon how he believed God was doing a new thing in their community and that he was grateful for the revival.

The head deacon, unfortunately, could not be easily persuaded.

As the crowds grew each night, this deacon's anger grew, as well. His militancy peaked when he actually threatened to burn the revival tent down if the pastor would not do something to "fix the problem." (The only person who saw a problem, however, was the deacon himself!)

The pastor was terribly broken and baffled by the deacon's behavior. He could not understand where all the hatefulness stemmed from. He told me, in fact, that this deacon was the largest supporter within the church of missionaries and orphanages in Africa. Things just didn't add up!

The pastor mustered up enough courage to ask the deacon himself how he could be so unloving. "Brother," he said, "This just doesn't make sense to me. Why would you give so much money to missions work in Africa yet not want the black people right here in your own community to be saved?"

His answer was surprising. "Pastor," he said, "that's exactly why I've always given so much to foreign missions. I don't mind black people who are in Africa. They're far away from me, thousands of miles away. I just don't want the ones here getting too close."

What a sad story! I learned a powerful lesson from this experience, though. While not all Christians struggle with issues of prejudice in their own lives, many Christians, like this deacon, do find it easier to love people who are far away and not so near.

Overseas missions are great and important. You'll never hear me trying to talk you out of sponsoring a child, helping support someone overseas, paying for the translation of God's Word into another language, or anything like that. But

my question for you is this: Are you matching your zeal for overseas missions with a zeal for walking in agape love each day? The real challenge is loving those around you each day—especially those who seem very "unlovable" at times.

God wants us to love people even when we don't feel like it. It is this kind of love, agape love, that fuels our faith and keeps us going strong in the faith walk. You can have all the other virtues to your name—faith, prophecy, tongues, giving—but if you miss "the love boat," then you've failed.

And now abide faith, hope, love, these three; but the greatest of these is love. (1 Corinthians 13:13)

DAY THIRTEEN

Faith means relying on God for our provision—not man.

Our heavenly Father is a very experienced
One. He knows very well that His children
wake up with a good appetite every morning....
He sustained 3 million Israelites in the wilder-
ness for 40 years. We do not expect He will
send 3 million missionaries to China; but if He
did, He would have ample means to sustain
them all....Depend on it, God's work done in
God's way will never lack God's supply.
—Hudson Taylor*

As human beings, one of the most difficult things to do is
not to worry. You know what I'm talking about. When
the money's tight, when our health is shaky, when our
loved ones are traveling, or when we're embarking on change

---

* Reprinted in *Our Daily Bread*, May 16, 1992. <http://www.
christianglobe.com/Illustrations/theDetails.asp?whichOne=p&wh
ichFile=provision> (18 June 2004)

in our lives, it's hard *not* to worry. Even when nothing out of the ordinary is happening at all—when everything is quiet, normal, and A-OK—we still seem to find reasons to worry. We are worrywarts by nature.

Our God knows this about us, and my guess is that that's why Jesus made sure to set some time aside for teaching about the habit of worrying. What was His lesson for us? In a nutshell, *Don't worry!*

This is definitely one of those things that are easier said than done. When your friend, who's been unemployed for months, comes to you nervous about a job interview he has tomorrow, it's easy enough for you to turn to him and say, "Don't worry." Those two small words, three syllables in all, don't take a lot of effort on your part. *Don't worry.* Simple enough.

> "Don't worry" is easier said than done.

But for your friend—the one who's facing the job interview, the fear of not getting the job, the possibility of having to live for who knows how much longer without a job, and the potential of not having enough money to pay for the electric bill that's due next week—*Don't worry* is one tall order.

But you see, when Jesus said, "Don't worry," that's not all He said. He didn't flippantly mumble, "Don't worry," and then walk away—as we are sometimes apt to do with those in need in our lives. Instead, He said, "Don't worry; My Father will take care of your needs," and then set to work comforting us with reminders of our Father's past provisions.

Therefore I say to you, do not worry about your life, what you will eat or what you will drink; nor about your body, what you will put on. Is not life more than food and the body more than clothing? Look at the birds of

the air, for they neither sow nor reap nor gather into barns; yet your heavenly Father feeds them. Are you not of more value than they? Which of you by worrying can add one cubit to his stature? So why do you worry about clothing? Consider the lilies of the field, how they grow: they neither toil nor spin; and yet I say to you that even Solomon in all his glory was not arrayed like one of these. Now if God so clothes the grass of the field, which today is, and tomorrow is thrown into the oven, will He not much more clothe you, O you of little faith? Therefore do not worry, saying, "What shall we eat?" or "What shall we drink?" or "What shall we wear?" For after all these things the Gentiles seek. For your heavenly Father knows that you need all these things. But seek first the kingdom of God and His righteousness, and all these things shall be added to you. Therefore do not worry about tomorrow, for tomorrow will worry about its own things. Sufficient for the day is its own trouble. (Matthew 6:25–34)

What a wonderful provider our God is! The reason we don't have to worry is because He has taken care of all our needs. If He can dress the flowers in their fancy clothes and make sure the birds have their suppers every night, certainly He can and will take care of His children's needs, as well!

I learned this lesson in a powerful way shortly after receiving my healing from cancer. Although I had been freed from the cancer, I soon found myself needing freedom in another realm—the financial realm. Because of the cancer, more than two years had passed since I'd worked a job. During this same time, hospital bills kept piling up. By the end of my illness, all the money in my savings was completely exhausted and I found myself more than one hundred thousand dollars in debt.

Days to Faith

I knew that I had to start earning an income—and fast! Right on time, God blessed me with my first preaching assignment since the illness. I remember not even having enough money to get to the meeting; I had to borrow a car and $100 from a friend just to make the trip down to Jonesboro, Arkansas, where I would be preaching at a small church for a weeklong revival.

I remember the church being jam-packed the first night. The sanctuary comfortably seated between ninety and a hundred people, but we had at least 150 every night. At the end of the week, they took an offering and gave me the $500 that had been collected. I knew that $500 was just a drop in my bucket of debt, but at least it was a start, and I was grateful for the provision.

But to my surprise, God told me to give all the money, all $500, to a little old lady who had been coming to the revival services faithfully each night. Let me tell you, this was not an easy thing to do. It certainly didn't feel good to hand over $500 that I knew I desperately needed. But you know what? God was teaching me a lesson through that experience, a lesson that I needed even more than that $500. That lesson was complete dependence on Him.

> God's provision is the antidote to worry.

Even though I felt like I needed the money far more than this lady did, I went ahead and did exactly what God had told me to do. I handed the money over. It turns out this woman owed $500 to the electric company—exactly the amount I gave her. In asking me to give the $500 to this woman, God allowed me to be part of His provision for this child of God. Without the $500, this woman would have had her electric services cut off that week.

Day Thirteen

Later on I came to realize that this woman had been walking in faithful obedience regarding money, as well. One night during the meeting, I distinctly recall receiving a faith offering for the church. This same woman had sown $70 in that offering—$70 that had initially been set aside to pay for the electric bill. When I gave her the offering, she wept with joy, realizing that God had answered her prayers.

I was doing a little weeping of my own, but for a totally different reason. I was weeping because the meeting was over and I didn't have the foggiest idea as to how I was going to get to my next speaking engagement. On the very last night before I left the meeting, a middle-aged man in the church handed me check for $1000. Talk about provision! The Lord greatly provided for my material needs that evening. Even more importantly, however, He provided for my spiritual needs by teaching me the necessity of relying on Him, even when I don't understand exactly what He's doing. That evening marked the beginning for me of a closer faith walk with God.

"Don't worry," our Lord says. "I have everything all taken care of."

Day Fourteen

The life of faith is not necessarily a life of ease.

Many times when individuals become Christians, they have the false notion that the life ahead of them is going to be smooth riding. Often that's the reason behind their decision to begin with. They feel stressed out, oppressed, overwhelmed, and downright discouraged by life. As soon as they hear promises of an "easy yoke" and a "light burden" (see Matthew 11:30), they're hopping onboard, sometimes even before you can extend the altar call.

Now don't get me wrong. I'm not trying to contradict Christ's words. He told us there is life and rest in Him, and any promise of Christ's is a promise we can take to the bank!

Come to Me, all you who labor and are heavy laden, and I will give you rest. Take My yoke upon you and learn from Me, for I am gentle and lowly in heart, and you will find rest for your souls. For My yoke is easy and My burden is light. (Matthew 11:28–30)

 40 Days to Faith

Where people go wrong, however, is in assuming that everything is going to be smooth sailing as soon as they start the Christian life. Nothing could be further from the truth. Christ Himself, in fact, devoted a lot of time during His earthly ministry preparing His followers for the demands of the Christian walk. One of the most poignant examples of this is found in the book of Luke.

> *Now it happened as they journeyed on the road, that someone said to Him, "Lord, I will follow You wherever You go." And Jesus said to him, "Foxes have holes and birds of the air have nests, but the Son of Man has nowhere to lay His head." Then He said to another, "Follow Me." But he said, "Lord, let me first go and bury my father." Jesus said to him, "Let the dead bury their own dead, but you go and preach the kingdom of God." And another also said, "Lord, I will follow You, but let me first go and bid them farewell who are at my house." But Jesus said to him, "No one, having put his hand to the plow, and looking back, is fit for the kingdom of God."*
> (Luke 9:57–62)

Three separate men came to Jesus wanting to follow Him, and Jesus made sure that each one understood the high cost of the commitment they were about to make. Not wanting them to make a decision in ignorance, He told them right up front all that would be required. "You must abandon all else for Me," He said. This was certainly not a "life of ease" He was calling them to.

The same holds true for us. When we signed up for lives of faith, we weren't signing up for luxury vacations. While it's true that we have the Holy Spirit as a Comforter to lead and guide is, it's not true that everything gets easier when we start to walk in faith. As Jesus' words in Luke reveal, frequently it actually gets harder.

Day Fourteen

Why is the faith life so hard? Well, for one thing, although Christ has redeemed and cleansed us from our sins, we still continue to struggle with them on a daily basis. Paul captured this internal struggle quite clearly in Romans.

For we know that the law is spiritual, but I am carnal, sold under sin. For what I am doing, I do not understand. For what I will to do, that I do not practice; but what I hate, that I do. If, then, I do what I will not to do, I agree with the law that it is good. But now, it is no longer I who do it, but sin that dwells in me. For I know that in me (that is, in my flesh) nothing good dwells; for to will is present with me, but how to perform what is good I do not find. For the good that I will to do, I do not do; but the evil I will not to do, that I practice. Now if I do what I will not to do, it is no longer I who do it, but sin that dwells in me. I find then a law, that evil is present with me, the one who wills to do good. For I delight in the law of God according to the inward man. But I see another law in my members, warring against the law of my mind, and bringing me into captivity to the law of sin which is in my members. O wretched man that I am! Who will deliver me from this body of death? (Romans 7:14–24)

What a tongue twister! Did you catch all that? Basically Paul was just commenting on the spiritual battle he found himself in every day. His renewed spirit, the *"new creation"* (2 Corinthians 5:17) in Christ, realized righteousness should have been his sole pursuit. As a sinful human being, however, he found himself being daily ensnared by his fleshly desires. That is what this verse is all about—the constant spiritual "back-and-forthing" each one of us finds ourselves in.

> Faith is not a luxury vacation.

For another thing, as servants of the Most High God, we automatically have bull's-eyes on our backs as far as the Enemy is concerned. Satan is like a roaring lion, prowling around in hopes of capturing us. Now the last time I checked, a life of constant running from a predatory cat was not to be considered as a "life of ease."

Another reason the life of faith is so hard, a reason that not many people think about, is that we so deeply desire to start living in our heavenly home. God blesses us in so many ways during our time here on earth, but even the most amazing earthly blessings are nothing compared to the eternal blessings God has waiting for us. Have you ever been about to go on vacation and the last week at home before you leave is practically torture? Every day seems to drag on because you want to hop on that plane, train, or automobile and get your vacation started ASAP! Paul expressed similar feelings to this in Philippians when he wrote,

> *For to me, to live is Christ, and to die is gain. But if I live on in the flesh, this will mean fruit from my labor; yet what I shall choose I cannot tell. For I am hard pressed between the two, having a desire to depart and be with Christ, which is far better.*
>
> (Philippians 1:21–23)

For Paul, being with Christ in heaven was far better than anything this earthly life had to offer, so much so that he could honestly say, *"to die is gain."* Maybe you're feeling the same. If you're truly growing in your faith, I guarantee you that there will be times when you'll feel the same—when you'll want more than anything for your life on earth to end so you can start your eternal life in heaven. As Paul said, though, *"to live is Christ."* In other words, although this life

is hard, we are to faithfully continue in it as laborers for the Lord.

Perhaps you're familiar with the popular 1970s and '80s television show *M*A*S*H*. I never really watched the show, but a friend recently shared with me an appropriate quote spoken by Father Mulcahy, the chaplain on *M*A*S*H*. "A faith of convenience," he said, "is a hollow faith."* How true! As we will see in a later chapter on the testing of our faith, only faith that has been through the ringer is really worthy of being called "faith."

No matter what anyone tells you, the Christian walk is not a life of ease. Faith, my friends, is not for the faint-hearted.

---

* Father Mulcahy, *M*A*S*H*, "A Holy Mess," 1982. <http://www.quotegarden.com/faith.html> (7 June 2004)

DAY FIFTEEN

Faith means acknowledging the sovereignty of God.

The book of Job chronicles the life story of a great hero of faith, a man who experienced more pain and loss than many of us will ever be called to face. In a relatively short amount of time, he lost his business, his possessions, his children, his health, and the support of his wife and friends. As Job lay miserable and sick in the ashes, his wife actually turned to him and said, *"Curse God and die!"* (Job 2:9). Can you imagine going through all that heartache—and, on top of it, having to go through it alone because those closest to you didn't understand what was going on?

Some people today falsely think that if Job was such a great man of faith, he wouldn't have gone through all the afflictions he did. Surely God must have been punishing him for something, they say. Well, you know what? Some of Job's closest friends thought the exact same thing. One friend, Eliphaz, basically said to him, "Job, what on earth did you do to make God so angry? You had better figure out fast and start repenting." To be exact, he said,

Is it for your piety that [God] rebukes you and brings charges against you? Is not your wickedness great? Are not your sins endless? You demanded security from your brothers for no reason; you stripped men of their clothing, leaving them naked. You gave no water to the weary and you withheld food from the hungry, though you were a powerful man, owning land—an honored man, living on it. And you sent widows away empty-handed and broke the strength of the fatherless. That is why snares are all around you, why sudden peril terrifies you, why it is so dark you cannot see, and why a flood of water covers you. (Job 22:4–11 NIV)

At the end of Job's suffering, however, God rebuked Eliphaz and the others for teaching wrong things about Him.

After the LORD had said these things to Job, he said to Eliphaz the Temanite, "I am angry with you and your two friends, because you have not spoken of me what is right, as my servant Job has. So now take seven bulls and seven rams and go to my servant Job and sacrifice a burnt offering for yourselves. My servant Job will pray for you, and I will accept his prayer and not deal with you according to your folly. You have not spoken of me what is right, as my servant Job has." (Job 42:7–8 NIV)

Surely, then, the book of Job does not teach that the faithful will never suffer, or that those who suffer must not have faith. On the contrary, because Job endured his afflictions the way he did, it validated his faith in God. Job's faithfulness in the midst of storms allowed God to prove how faithful He really is.

Let's take a closer look at Job's life. First off, we know that he was a man of great faith from the opening pages of his story. The very first verse of the book introduces Job as a

"man [who] was blameless and upright, and one who feared God and shunned evil" (Job 1:1). In addition to that, we find God boasting about Job to Satan. You heard me right: Like a thrilled parent, God was showing off Job.

> *Now there was a day when the sons of God came to present themselves before the LORD, and Satan also came among them. And the LORD said to Satan, "From where do you come?" So Satan answered the LORD and said, "From going to and fro on the earth, and from walking back and forth on it." Then the LORD said to Satan, "Have you considered My servant Job, that there is none like him on the earth, a blameless and upright man, one who fears God and shuns evil?"* (Job 1:6–8)

You know you have reached the pinnacle of your faith walk when God can recommend you as one of His trophies, and that is precisely what happened with Job. But if Job was so faithful, then why did he have to go through so much heartache? This is precisely what Job was wondering throughout his whole ordeal. "I'm innocent," he kept asserting, "so why am I being put through the ringer, God?"

God's ways are not man's ways.

While Job never got a direct answer to this question, he learned a few lessons far more important—namely, that God's ways are not man's ways and that the faithful are called to rest on God's sovereignty even (and especially) in the midst of chaos.

Job very easily could have taken his wife's advice by choosing to *"curse God and die!"* Thank goodness he didn't. Instead, he constantly reminded himself of who actually was in charge. This is the key to you lasting and staying strong in faith, no matter what. You lose your home, but instead

of despairing, you remind yourself, "God is still in charge." Your children turn to drugs and crime, yet you keep repeating the truth, "God is in charge, even in this." No matter what life brings, you can choose—just as Job chose—to keep your eyes on the prize and keep pressing on.

God is sovereign. No matter how chaotic and out of control your life may seem here at times, absolutely everything, down to the smallest little detail, is 100 percent in His hands. What a mighty God we serve! Praise Him for His sovereignty!

DAY SIXTEEN

Faith is being sure of what we hope for.

Perhaps one of the single best places to go in the Bible for a definition of faith is Hebrews 11. In the very first verse of this chapter, the writer of Hebrews said faith is *"the substance of things hoped for, the evidence of things not seen."* You can't get any clearer than that. Right there, in Hebrews 1:1, the Holy Spirit gives us a clear definition of faith: *"the substance of things hoped for,"* and *"the evidence of things not seen."* I'd like to first turn our attention to the beginning part of this verse, where the writer said faith is *"the substance of things hoped for."* We'll talk about *"the evidence of things not seen"* in a later chapter.

So, what did the writer mean when he said faith is *"the substance of things hoped for"*? The *New International Version* translates the verse like this: *"Faith is being sure of what we hope for."* In other words, faith and hope have an element of confidence to them, of *"being sure."* In other words, when you say you have faith or hope in something, you're saying, "I am certain that this is true."

Nowadays in the secular world, the word hope has come to mean something entirely different. People will express "hope" in winning the lottery. A teenage girl might "hope" her crush will ask her to the prom. The word *hope* in such instances is used to express a wish or desire more than confidence or certainty.

Christian hope is an anchor for the soul.

Biblical hope, however, is much more valuable, for it is certain. When you practice biblical hope, you can be confident you'll get what you're hoping for. Whereas the person hoping to win the lottery probably expects not to, the person putting hope in Jesus Christ confidently expects all the blessings that such a hope provides.

Since faith means being sure of what we hope for, let's take a closer look at the biblical definition of hope. Here are some verses to consider.

First, as we've already discussed, hope is certain. When it comes to things of the kingdom, we can be confident that our hope is solid and unshakable:

Now hope does not disappoint, because the love of God has been poured out in our hearts by the Holy Spirit who was given to us. (Romans 5:5)

Our hope is so confident, in fact, that Scripture also refers to it as *"an anchor of the soul."* Clearly, biblical hope is not wishy-washy in the least!

This hope we have as an anchor of the soul, *both sure and steadfast, and which enters the Presence behind the veil, where the forerunner has entered for us, even*

Jesus, having become High Priest forever according to the order of Melchizedek.
(Hebrews 6:19–20, emphasis added)

What exactly is this soul-anchoring hope in? According to God's Word, our hope is the very salvation of our souls and the eternal life that awaits us:

*But let us who are of the day be sober, putting on the breastplate of faith and love, **and as a helmet the hope of salvation.*** (1 Thessalonians 5:8, emphasis added)

*But when the kindness and the love of God our Savior toward man appeared, not by works of righteousness which we have done, but according to His mercy He saved us, through the washing of regeneration and renewing of the Holy Spirit, whom He poured out on us abundantly through Jesus Christ our Savior, that having been justified by His grace **we should become heirs according to the hope of eternal life.***
(Titus 3:4–7, emphasis added)

*For I consider that the sufferings of this present time are not worthy to be compared with the glory which shall be revealed in us. **For the earnest expectation of the creation eagerly waits for the revealing of the sons of God. For the creation was subjected to futility, not willingly, but because of Him who subjected it in hope; because the creation itself also will be delivered from the bondage of corruption into the glorious liberty of the children of God.** For we know that the whole creation groans and labors with birth pangs together until now. Not only that, but we also who have the firstfruits of the Spirit, even we ourselves groan within ourselves, eagerly waiting for the adoption, the redemption of our body. **For we were saved***

in this hope, but hope that is seen is not hope; for why does one still hope for what he sees? But if we hope for what we do not see, we eagerly wait for it with perseverance.

(Romans 8:18–25, emphasis added)

This dual hope of salvation and eternal life in heaven is only available because of the sacrificial death and resurrection of Jesus Christ, our Lord. And it's not available to everyone, either—only to those who accept the hope in faith. You see, faith and hope go hand-in-hand. They cannot be separated. It is only through faith that we can ever attain the things we hope for.

We through the Spirit eagerly wait for the hope of righteousness by faith. (Galatians 5:5)

Where does our hope come from? Just like faith, hope is a gift from God, and we learn about this gift of hope and all that it entails through His Word:

*We give thanks to the God and Father of our Lord Jesus Christ, praying always for you, since we heard of your faith in Christ Jesus and of your love for all the saints; because of **the hope which is laid up for you in heaven, of which you heard before in the word of the truth of the gospel.***

(Colossians 1:3–5, emphasis added)

*And you, who once were alienated and enemies in your mind by wicked works, yet now He has reconciled in the body of His flesh through death, to present you holy, and blameless, and above reproach in His sight—if indeed you continue in the faith, grounded and steadfast, and are not moved away from **the hope of the gospel which you heard, which was preached***

__to every creature under heaven,__ of which I, Paul, became a minister.

(Colossians 1:21–23, emphasis added)

I pray this brief look at hope has helped you to better understand what it means to have faith, for we can't truly have faith unless we first know what we're hoping for. Do you have the hope—or confident expectation—of salvation in Jesus Christ and eternal life with Him in heaven?

DAY SEVENTEEN

Faith is infectious.

One of the things I have come to discover during my years as a Christian is that people who operate in faith tend to activate, or set off, faith in others. What results is a chain reaction, or domino effect, as heightened faith gets passed down the line from one person to the next.

This is one reason why it's so important to surround yourself with people who walk by faith. Their faith walk will eventually rub off and positively influence you. Such was the case with the prophet Elijah and the widow woman he met in Zarepath.

God specifically spoke to Elijah, telling him to go to a Phoenician city called Zarephath, where a widowed woman would care for him.

> *Then the word of the LORD came to him, saying, "Arise, go to Zarephath, which belongs to Sidon, and dwell there. See, I have commanded a widow there to provide for you."* (1 Kings 17:8–9)

Elijah, like the good prophet and man of God that he was, immediately obeyed and headed for the city. As expected, he found things as the Lord had said they would be. *"So he arose and went to Zarephath. And when he came to the gate of the city, indeed a widow was there gathering sticks"* (1 Kings 17:10).

Now I can only imagine what might have been going through Elijah's head at this point. God told him the widow in Zarephath would provide for him—but this woman was poor! How was she going to care for him when she could barely care for herself?

Isn't this just like God—to use someone who seems least capable so that He will get all the glory instead of man? Elijah could have doubted what God was doing at this point, or even wondered if God was playing some kind of joke on him. "God, why have you sent me to a poor widow woman who has nothing?" he could have asked.

> Faith can rub off and influence others.

But instead, Elijah stepped out in faith. "God said this woman would provide for me," Elijah thought, "so we had better get this show started!" In faith, he asked her for some water and food:

And he called to her and said, "Please bring me a little water in a cup, that I may drink." And as she was going to get it, he called to her and said, "Please bring me a morsel of bread in your hand." (verses 10–11)

Immediately the widow woman explained that she did not have enough food to share.

So she said, "As the LORD your God lives, I do not have bread, only a handful of flour in a bin, and a little oil in a jar; and see, I am gathering a couple of sticks that I may go

*in and prepare it for myself and my son, that we may eat it,
and die."* (1 Kings 17:12)

Once again, we see how poor this woman was. She and
her son were down to their very last meal—not their last meal
of the day, or the month, or the year. The last meal of their lives!
After this, they were preparing to die. This woman was in a sad,
sad state.

Elijah, in faith, knew this situation was not too big for the
Lord. God had promised, after all, that this widow would provide for him! Yet again, Elijah took a bold step of faith:

*And Elijah said to her, "Do not fear; go and do as you have
said, but make me a small cake from it first, and bring it to
me; and afterward make some for yourself and your son.
For thus says the LORD God of Israel: 'The bin of flour shall
not be used up, nor shall the jar of oil run dry, until the day
the LORD sends rain on the earth.'"* (verses 13–14)

Had this woman chosen to walk in the flesh, she probably
would have ignored Elijah and turned her attention back to preparing her final meal. This is what conventional wisdom would
have told her to do. "Ignore the prophet, and just enjoy your last
meal," the carnal mind-set would have said.

The widowed woman, however, had "caught" some of Elijah's faith. Seeing the confidence with which he trusted God,
she began wondering if this faith thing might be worth a try.
And so, instead of responding in the flesh, she responded in
faith:

*She went away and did according to the word of Elijah;
and she and he and her household ate for many days.
The bin of flour was not used up, nor did the jar of oil run
dry, according to the word of the LORD which He spoke by
Elijah.* (1 Kings 17:15–16)

Do you see the wonderful principal of infectious faith woven throughout this story? It was because of Elijah's confident faith that the widowed woman chose to walk in faith herself. Just a short time later, Elijah had the opportunity to practice this "infectious faith" for the widow's benefit again. Her son had died, and understandably, she was broken. She was so distraught, in fact, that she yelled at Elijah, *"What have I to do with you, O man of God? Have you come to me to bring my sin to remembrance, and to kill my son?"* (verse 18). This woman was upset!

Elijah didn't miss a beat. He immediately set out to handle the situation in faith.

> *And he said to her, "Give me your son." So he took him out of her arms and carried him to the upper room where he was staying, and laid him on his own bed. Then he cried out to the LORD and said, "O LORD my God, have You also brought tragedy on the widow with whom I lodge, by killing her son?" And he stretched himself out on the child three times, and cried out to the LORD and said, "O LORD my God, I pray, let this child's soul come back to him." Then the LORD heard the voice of Elijah; and the soul of the child came back to him, and he revived.* (verses 19–22)

Once again, Elijah's faith was rewarded. And once again, Elijah's infectious faith spread.

> *Then the woman said to Elijah, "Now by this I know that you are a man of God, and that the word of the LORD in your mouth is the truth."* (verse 24)

Are you practicing infectious faith? And please understand, by infectious, I don't mean obnoxious. So frequently I see Christians mix these two up. They think the only way to show their faith is by wearing Christian T-shirts all the time, singing their favorite Bible songs at the top of their lungs

everywhere they go, and plastering their cars with "Jesus Loves You" bumper stickers. Nothing, however, could be further from the truth.

The best way to practice infectious faith is simply to obey. In Elijah's case, for instance, the spread of faith started when Elijah asked for food and water, just as the Lord had commanded him. This request for food wasn't grand, dramatic, super-spiritual, or showy. It was just obedience in action.

So, let me ask you again: Are you practicing infectious faith? Are you daily walking in obedience while trusting the Lord to use your faithfulness to incite faith in others? It is my prayer that you will come to a point where you can answer these questions with a resounding, "Yes!"

Day Eighteen

Faith means looking at things in the spiritual, not the natural.

For as long as I live, I will never forget the initial feeling that came over me when the doctor told me, in plain and simple language, that there was nothing more they could do. "Mr. Coe," he said, "I am sorry to have to tell you this, but you're not going to make it. The cancer has spread so rapidly through your body that there is really nothing more we can do about it." The devastation I felt in hearing those words was like a ton of bricks crushing my body. A feeling of nausea took over my gut. I felt totally deluded, depressed, and abandoned.

At the time, I was in my early forties. My father had died at the young age of thirty-eight many years before. Because of my father's death, many people assumed an early death might be in store for me as well. From a natural standpoint, it looked like I was doomed.

The severity of my case didn't make things any better. If the cancer had been confined to one area, things still would have been bad—but much more manageable. The cancer

in my body, however, had pretty much taken over, affecting my kidneys, my colon, and my liver. All three of those areas are tremendously important for survival. Without healthy kidneys to properly remove uric acid and waste materials, a healthy colon to excrete solid waste, and a healthy liver to filter blood, I was basically on a downhill course.

Needless to say, I was experiencing a great amount of despair, despair that continued for several days. At that point in my life, I had not even started to tap into the potential that God placed within me. My mind was confused as I wrestled with my death verdict, because I clearly remembered God telling me He would use me in a mighty way to do His work. But how could He use me to spread His Word on earth if I wasn't even on it?

We need to see through spiritual lenses instead of earthbound eyes.

As I was wrestling with all of this, God dramatically got hold of my attention. "Why are you looking at everything in the natural," He seemed to be saying, "when I've called you to live on a much greater plane?" Suddenly, I began to realize that God did indeed have a master plan to keep me alive.

I didn't know exactly how His plan would unfold at that point in time, but I did know that He had something special in store. He had promised to use me for His work, and I knew He always keeps His promises. Even if it meant preaching from my deathbed while preparing to enter through the pearly gates of heaven, so be it! If God promised to use me, then He would use me in one form or another.

As I began to dwell on this fact instead of the death sentence that had been pronounced over me, my feelings of despair started to lift and lighten. My problem was that

Day Eighteen

I had become so focused on the physical facts around me that I'd forgotten the much more important spiritual realm. The spiritual realm is an unseen realm, so no wonder it's easy to forget sometimes. As children of faith, however, God has commanded us to live on this spiritual plane, to evaluate all of life through spiritual lenses instead of earthbound eyes.

> *We do not look at the things which are seen, but at the things which are not seen. For the things which are seen are temporary, but the things which are not seen are eternal.* (2 Corinthians 4:18)

God, in His graciousness, used my sickness to jolt my attention back to the unseen, spiritual realm. In my case, once I began focusing on the eternal and not temporal, God assured me that my life on earth would not end with that cancer. Had I not been healed, however, it still would have been my duty to focus and dwell upon eternal things. Instead of spending all my time worrying and wondering why my body wasn't getting better, for instance, I could have used the experience to share the message of Christ with the doctors and fellow patients around me. "See how fast this body's giving way?" I might have said. "Well, thank God I've got a better one waiting for me on the other side of eternity." You'd be amazed how little comments like this open the door to great opportunities for sharing your faith.

The eyes of faith are always turning to the eternal, unseen realm. Are you thinking on the eternal, unseen things of God? Or are your thoughts stuck on the temporary, fleeting things of earth? It's my prayer that your heart's eyes will be on heaven in every moment of every day.

DAY NINETEEN

Faith is just the starting point for spiritual growth.

I hope that, if nothing else, this book will impress upon your heart the important role faith plays in the Christian life. I pray that as you study more about faith in God's Word, you will grow in that faith and in your faithfulness to the things of God. Faith is a wonderful gift from God, and as we learn to walk in it more fully, the results are amazing.

No matter how important faith is, however, we need to realize that it is just the starting point for spiritual growth. Many Christians treat faith as the "end all, be all," the only aim of the Christian walk. They seem to have the idea that, as soon as they've started walking in faith, they have no more spiritual growth to do. "As long as I have faith," they say, "what more is there?"

Oh, my friends, there is so much more! Once we have started implementing faith in our lives, it's not time to retire. On the contrary, when you start walking in faith, you're just getting started for the exciting Christian walk ahead!

One of my favorite Scripture passages, one that God has used mightily to get through to my spirit, is found in 2 Peter 1. The Holy Spirit, through Peter, wrote the following:

Simon Peter, a bondservant and apostle of Jesus Christ, To those who have obtained like precious faith with us by the righteousness of our God and Savior Jesus Christ....For this very reason, giving all diligence, add to your faith virtue, to virtue knowledge, to knowledge self-control, to self-control perseverance, to persever-ance godliness, to godliness brotherly kindness, and to brotherly kindness love. For if these things are yours and abound, you will be neither barren nor unfruitful in the knowledge of our Lord Jesus Christ.

(2 Peter 1:1, 5–8)

There's a whole lot of meat packed into these few short verses! Let's start at the beginning. Peter said that he was writing *"to those who have obtained like precious faith with us."* In other words, he was talking to Christians who are already walking the faith walk. Since faith is not the "end all, be all" in the Christian life, Peter went on to tell his readers the things they must be sure to *"add"* to their faith.

In other words, don't think you've reached your final spiritual mountaintop just because you have faith. God has a whole lot of lessons still in store for you! What kind of lessons? Well, to list a few,

- *"virtue,"* or the good things of God
- *"knowledge,"* or understanding of God's Word and His ways
- *"temperance,"* or self-control in all your actions, words, and thoughts

- *"patience,"* or the persevering, stick-with-it attitude that endures hardships without complaining
- *"godliness,"* or a Christlike spirit
- *"brotherly kindness,"* or a polite, gentle spirit to your brothers and sisters in Christ
- *"charity,"* or deep, self-sacrificing, agape love

One thing that's often overlooked in this passage is a small, three-word phrase found at the start of verse five. Peter wrote that we are to add all these things to our faith by *"giving all diligence."* In other words, we aren't supposed to just wander through life, hoping to stumble upon virtue, knowledge, temperance, patience, godliness, brotherly kindness, and charity. On the contrary, we are to actively, intentionally, and diligently seek after these spiritual building blocks.

> We need to be intentional about spiritual growth.

Have you contented yourself to stay where you are in faith? Or are you pushing forward in spiritual growth as the Lord has called you to do? I challenge you to seek after and implement these qualities in your life. Add them to your faith, as the Lord has instructed us!

Just like faith, though, these are not things we can handle on our own. Our faith is a gift from God, and so is every one these attributes. Start out with prayer. Pray specifically for virtue, knowledge, temperance, patience, godliness, brotherly kindness, and charity. Devote a week, a month, or even a whole year to focusing on and developing each of these qualities. Depending on your spiritual strengths and weaknesses, some qualities might take longer than others to develop, but don't get discouraged. Just keep at it.

Day Twenty

Untested faith is not faith enough.

My brethren, count it all joy when you fall into various trials, knowing that the testing of your faith produces patience. But let patience have its perfect work, that you may be perfect and complete, lacking nothing.
—James 1:2–4

Nobody likes tests. Most students dread the exams that they must take throughout the school year. A sick patient doesn't look forward to the blood tests, stress tests, and other medical testing procedures he must go through to find out what's wrong with his health. And nobody naturally welcomes the many tests and trials that life frequently sends our way.

James told us here, however, that we are not just to endure these tests and trials—we are actually to *"count* [them] *all joy"*! This is one tall order. How do we train ourselves to accept testing with joy?

Before we address this question, however, I want us to realize an important point: No one is exempt from being tested. If you are a man or woman of God walking in faith, then you can count on your faith being tested at some point—if not at many points—along the way. So don't think you can ignore the command in James 1:2–4 because it doesn't apply to you. If you're walking in faith, you're going to face trials. Period.

Every faithful man and woman of the Bible went through at least one season of testing. Consider "the hall of faith" found in Hebrews 11. Every single person in that chapter made it on "faith's honor roll" because his or her faith was tested and did not break.

Here is just a glimpse at some of the tests and trials God's faithful followers have had to face throughout history:

- THE TEST: Abraham was told he would be the father of many nations, yet his wife, Sarah, was barren and beyond childbearing years.

- THE TESTS: While walking in obedience to God, Joseph was sold by his own brothers into slavery. Once established in his new master's house, he was wrongly accused of rape and subsequently imprisoned for years.

- THE TEST: The New Testament believers, or "the people of the Way" as they were called, left everything and endured great persecution to follow their resurrected Savior, the Lord Jesus Christ. Crucifixions and stonings were not uncommon.

- THE TESTS: Jesus Christ, our Lord and Savior, endured the greatest tests of all—from His temptations in the desert to His intense and tiring

years of ministry, from His spiritual anguish in the garden of Gethsemane to ultimate spiritual and physical anguish of the cross, Jesus was no stranger to testing and trials:

He is despised and rejected by men, a Man of sorrows and acquainted with grief. And we hid, as it were, our faces from Him; He was despised, and we did not esteem Him. Surely He has borne our griefs and carried our sorrows; yet we esteemed Him stricken, smitten by God, and afflicted. But He was wounded for our transgressions, He was bruised for our iniquities; the chastisement for our peace was upon Him, and by His stripes we are healed. (Isaiah 53:3–5)

Christ Jesus,...being in the form of God, did not consider it robbery to be equal with God, but made Himself of no reputation, taking the form of a bondservant, and coming in the likeness of men. And being found in appearance as a man, He humbled Himself and became obedient to the point of death, even the death of the cross. (Philippians 2:5–8)

What I am trying to get you to understand is that no matter who you are, your faith will be tested and tried in the furnace of life. To return to our question from earlier, how do we learn to *"count it all joy"* (James 1:2) when we find ourselves amidst these fiery trials? Believe it or not, the answer is found in this very same passage. Let's read it again:

*My brethren, count it all joy when you fall into various trials, **knowing that the testing of your faith produces patience.** But let patience have its perfect work, that you may be perfect and complete, lacking nothing.* (James 1:2–4, emphasis added)

Is it starting to make sense? We can count our tests as joys because we know testing produces patience in our lives. And patience, when it's allowed to do its work, makes us *"perfect and complete."* The benefits of testing certainly sound worthwhile!

You see, untested faith is not really faith enough. When your faith is tested, you are refined in the process. You begin to reflect a clearer image of Jesus Christ. If Christ's faith was tested, how much more do we need to be tested? Testing validates your testimony, proves your convictions, and prepares you to share your faith with others.

> If you're walking in faith, tests are inevitable.

Someone recently shared a quote with me by A. B. Simpson on the benefits of trials. He wrote,

> You will have no test of faith that will not fit you to be a blessing if you are obedient to the Lord. I never had a trial but when I got out of the deep river I found some poor pilgrim on the bank that I was able to help by that very experience. *

It is a bit difficult to convey your sympathy and understanding to someone when you've never experienced anything like what they're going through. It speaks volumes, however, when you can say, "I know you can make it. I went through the same fire, and the Lord brought me out not only alive, but as a victor!"

Ultimately, the tests are always for God's glory. When we go through the fire and come out purer and stronger than before, our Lord is greatly glorified:

*A.B.Simpson. <http://www.christianglobe.com/Illustrations/theDetails.asp?whichOne=t&whichFile=trials> (June 16 2004)

Day Twenty

Behold, I have refined you, but not as silver; I have tested you in the furnace of affliction. For My own sake, for My own sake, I will do it; for how should My name be profaned? And I will not give My glory to another.

(Isaiah 48:10–11)

He alone gets all glory for the good He brings out of our testing and trials. Praise God for His wonderful mysteries!

Day Twenty-One

Faith does NOT mean testing God.

W hile most Christians understand that the walk of faith requires testing, some are confused about who is giving the test. They forget the verses that clearly tell us we are NOT to test our God, verses like this one:

> *Do not test the LORD your God as you did at Massah.*
> (Deuteronomy 6:16 NIV)

What does testing the Lord look like? Let me give you a few examples.

There's a preacher I know of in the New England area who really loves the Lord. He's a first class soulwinner with a street ministry that's second to none. God is using him in a mighty way, and it's a joy to see the work being done through this man of great faith.

However, this preacher does have problems when it comes to the issue of testing God, particularly in the realm of healing. He often tells people things like, "I've got so much faith in God that I can walk around barefoot in a

snowstorm for hours and not get sick. God will protect me."

Recently we got a snowstorm in Texas, which doesn't happen very often. Let me tell you, the weather was cold! A snowstorm requires temperatures that are close to the freezing point. Yes, folks, that's around thirty-two degrees Fahrenheit. It makes me shiver all over again just thinking about it. But this pastor frequently "tests" God by exposing his body to extreme temperatures and consequently endangering his health. What ever happened to protecting the temple of the Holy Spirit? Did this pastor forget all about Romans 12?

Please believe me when I tell you that I'm not trying to make fun of this brother. He is extremely sincere in his convictions. The problem is that many of these convictions simply do not line up with the Word of God. This brother should not expect God-sent healings to follow such presumptuous acts. When we put God to the test and demand that He save us from our own asinine behavior, God is by no means obligated to perform healings on our behalf. For the most part, this brother was doing nothing more than tempting God. And what did Jesus say? *"It is written again, 'You shall not tempt the Lord your God'"* (Matthew 4:7).

> It's God's job to test us, not vice versa.

"But Brother Coe," you might be saying, "God uses the foolish things of the world to confound the wise—isn't that what the Word says?" Yes, you're absolutely right. But although God uses foolish things to confound the wise, He doesn't need you to supply any foolishness. It's your job to use rational judgment when it comes to health. Protect your temple of the Holy Spirit. God never tells a person to risk his or her life so that He'll have an opportunity to perform

a miracle. Let God take care of creating the miracle situations. You don't need to fabricate them.

One of the key ways we can avoid falling into the trap of "testing" God is by exercising self-control in our own lives. The Bible tells us several times that we are to seek after self-control:

> *But the fruit of the Spirit is love, joy, peace, longsuffering, kindness, goodness, faithfulness, gentleness, self-control. Against such there is no law.*
> (Galatians 5:22–23)

> *Add to your faith virtue, to virtue knowledge, to knowledge self-control, to self-control perseverance, to perseverance godliness, to godliness brotherly kindness, and to brotherly kindness love.* (2 Peter 1:5–7)

The following story is a clear example of how a lack of self-control can translate into a defiant testing of God. There was a lady who was instantly healed from a long battle with diabetes by the power of God in a healing meeting. She went to her doctor to confirm that the diabetes was in fact gone. The doctor was amazed to discover that, for the first time in more than thirteen years, this woman's blood sugar readings were actually normal. The physician concluded that she had received nothing short of a miracle.

When she came back to the healing meeting the next evening, she testified about what Christ had done in miraculously healing her. Just as everyone thought this woman was winding down her story and getting ready to take her seat, she went on to say more.

"I've got one more thing to share," she said. "Brothers and sisters in Christ, I want to let you know that I was so happy from receiving my miracle that I celebrated by eating

a whole pecan pie all by myself. Saints, I've wanted to do that for years, but with the high dosages of insulin I had to take each day, I knew that eating such a sugar-loaded dessert could kill me. But today I ate it all, and I am here to report that it was so good. I plan to eat a whole pecan pie at least once a week from now on. To God be the glory!"

While this woman had clearly received a healing from the Lord, her indulgence and lack of self-control evidenced an attitude of testing God. "How big of a miracle will you give me Lord?" she essentially asked with each pecan pie eaten. God didn't give her healing so that she could relapse into an unhealthy lifestyle. If anything, she should have been showing her gratitude to God by pursuing healthy eating habits!

Now understand, I'm no health freak out to preach a "do and do not eat" gospel; however, I do realize that if you are challenged in a certain area, you must choose to exercise a certain amount of self-control. Lack of self-control in any area will inevitably cause your life to become unfruitful.

Faith always has an element of testing, but remember that God is always the One who's testing. It's not our job to test the Lord, and to do so saddens our Father's heart.

Day Twenty-Two

Faith means moving forward when we can't see what's next.

R emember our definition of faith as found in Hebrews 11:1? *"Now faith is the substance of things hoped for, the evidence of things not seen."* We've already talked about the hope aspect; now it's time to turn our attention to "the evidence of things not seen."

What was the writer of Hebrews saying here? He was saying that we won't always be able to see—with our physical eyes—what's lying up ahead. We don't see heaven yet, for instance, but that doesn't lessen our confidence that it exists. By faith, we accept and affirm that it is a real place where we'll one day be.

Since faith always shows itself in action, and since we can't always see the object of our faith, there's an important conclusion to be drawn from this verse: Sometimes faith means moving forward when we can't see what's up ahead.

The world's wisdom says, "I'll believe it when I see it." Biblical wisdom, however, says, "I'll see it when I believe

it." Faith people are in a class of their own when it comes to envisioning things. We can look at raw, undeveloped land with seemingly little potential and see it as the future world head-quarters of a thriving evangelistic ministry. We can look at a life torn apart by drugs, violence, abuse, and anger, and picture it renewed, redeemed, and transformed by the blood of the Lamb. We can look at our own faltering Christian walks and envision the glorious, angst-free eternity that awaits us: *"He who has begun a good work in you will complete it until the day of Jesus Christ"* (Philippians 1:6).

> We can't always see what's coming next, but God can.

Isn't it hard to keep moving forward when we can't see what's coming next? If you've ever tried walking down the street, or around your house, or anywhere for that matter, with your eyes closed, you know that moving forward when you can't see what's up ahead is not the easiest thing to do. It can be downright scary at times, in fact!

No matter how frightening it may be to move forward in faith when we can't see what's next, there's a wonderful truth that provides comfort and confidence as we continue along. That truth is this: While we can't see what's coming up next, our Lord can.

An illustration was shared with me recently that helps illus-trate this point. A house caught fire one night, and a young boy inside was forced to seek temporary refuge on the roof. The boy's father, having already escaped from the fire, tried saving his son by standing on the ground below with open arms and calling for him to jump. "Jump!" he said over and over. "I will catch you. I promise."

From where the father stood, he could see the situation very clearly. As he watched the flames move toward his son, he knew

his son would have to jump in order to survive. The boy, understandably, was frightened. All he could see was fire, smoke, and blackness. The thought of jumping into the unknown terrified him almost as much as the thought of staying in the smoke.

The father continued his cries to the son: "Jump!" he said, over and over. "I will catch you!" The boy, however, protested. "Daddy, I can't see you," he said.

The father, without missing a beat, replied to the boy, "Yes, my son, but I can see you, and that's all that really matters."*

Faith means moving forward when we can't always see what's next. No matter how dark the unknown may seem, it's never unknown to our Lord. He is ahead, planning and guiding. He sees what's next, and He is sure to lead and protect us as we move forward into uncharted territories.

---

* <http://www.christianglobe.com/Illustrations/theDetails.asp?which One=f&whichFile=fait> (16 June 2004)

DAY TWENTY-THREE

A heritage of faith is a gift from God.

D id you know that even after you're gone from this earth and are safe in your eternal heavenly home, your faith can keep moving here on earth?

This is one of the greatest things about faith. When you physically die, faith doesn't. Like that pink Energizer Bunny® on TV, it can keep going and going and going and going. How? Because if you're a good steward of the faith God's given you, you make sure to pass it on to your descendants.

Scripture talks time and time again about the ongoing nature of faith. The Psalmist, for instance, reminded us that children themselves are *"a heritage from the LORD."* How much more so are children who walk in the same faith that we walk in!

Behold, children are a heritage from the LORD, the fruit of the womb is a reward. Like arrows in the hand of a warrior, so are the children of one's youth.

(Psalm 127:3–4)

Throughout Exodus, as God gave the Law to His people, He made sure to remind them of the generational nature of faith. With each new call to faithfulness, He commanded Israel to pass that faithfulness on to the generations that followed them:

> *And the other lamb you shall offer at twilight; and you shall offer with it the grain offering and the drink offering, as in the morning, for a sweet aroma, an offering made by fire to the LORD.* ***This shall be a continual burnt offering throughout your generations*** *at the door of the tabernacle of meeting before the LORD, where I will meet you to speak with you. And there I will meet with the children of Israel, and the tabernacle shall be sanctified by My glory.*
>
> (Exodus 29:41–43, emphasis added)

> *Work shall be done for six days, but the seventh is the Sabbath of rest, holy to the LORD. Whoever does any work on the Sabbath day, he shall surely be put to death.* ***Therefore the children of Israel shall keep the Sabbath, to observe the Sabbath throughout their generations as a perpetual covenant.*** *It is a sign between Me and the children of Israel forever; for in six days the LORD made the heavens and the earth, and on the seventh day He rested and was refreshed.*
>
> (Exodus 31:15–17, emphasis added)

Some of Moses' last words to Israel were on the heritage nature of faith. In his final blessing on the nation, he reminded them that God's Law and the faith they walked in were legacies passed on from their faithful father Jacob:

> *Yes, He loves the people; all His saints are in Your hand; they sit down at Your feet; everyone receives Your words. Moses commanded a law for us, a heritage of*

the congregation of Jacob. And He was King in Jeshurun, when the leaders of the people were gathered, all the tribes of Israel together. (Deuteronomy 33:3–5)

The Psalmist commented on heritage faith when he said that one generation should sing the Lord's praises to another:

One generation shall praise Your works to another, and shall declare Your mighty acts. (Psalm 145:4)

A poignant New Testament example of a legacy of faith is seen in the life of Timothy. When Paul wrote him in one of his letters, he praised God for Timothy's faith—a faith that had been handed down to him from his mother and grandmother:

Will you leave a heritage of faith or unfaith?

I thank God, whom I serve with a pure conscience, as my forefathers did, as without ceasing I remember you in my prayers night and day, greatly desiring to see you, being mindful of your tears, that I may be filled with joy, when I call to remembrance the genuine faith that is in you, which dwelt first in your grandmother Lois and your mother Eunice, and I am persuaded is in you also. (2 Timothy 1:3–5)

On the opposite side of the coin, if we abandon our faith, we leave behind a sad heritage for our offspring—a heritage of unfaith. The prophet Hosea talked about just such an inheritance when he berated the children of Israel for abandoning pure worship of the Most High God:

They have dealt treacherously with the LORD, for they have begotten pagan children. Now a New Moon shall devour them and their heritage. (Hosea 5:7)

As Moses reminded the children of Israel in Exodus, we've been given a choice. We can either pass our faith on to our offspring and ensure the blessings and joys in their lives that come from serving the Lord, or we can pass on unfaithfulness and disobedience—ensuring lifetimes of sadness and punishment in the generations that follow after us:

> *You shall not make for yourself a carved image, or any likeness of anything that is in heaven above, or that is in the earth beneath, or that is in the water under the earth; you shall not bow down to them nor serve them. For I, the LORD your God, am a jealous God, visiting the iniquity of the fathers upon the children to the third and fourth generations of those who hate Me, but showing mercy to thousands, to those who love Me and keep My commandments.* (Exodus 20:4–6)

Oh, that we would ensure blessings for our offspring instead of the curses of unfaith! It is my prayer that you would choose today to leave a heritage of faith for those who follow after you.

DAY TWENTY-FOUR

Faith is to be shared.

As important as it is to leave a legacy of faith to our offspring, our faith-sharing duties do not end there. God's Word clearly tells us time and again that we are to share the good news of His righteousness, justice, love, and mercy with those we encounter—whether they're family, friends, acquaintances, or enemies.

> *And Jesus came and spoke to them, saying, "All authority has been given to Me in heaven and on earth. Go therefore and make disciples of all the nations, baptizing them in the name of the Father and of the Son and of the Holy Spirit, teaching them to observe all things that I have commanded you; and lo, I am with you always, even to the end of the age."*
> (Matthew 28:18–20)

The Scriptures are filled with examples of men and women who shared their faith with those around them. The psalmist, for instance, spoke of God's faithfulness to *"the great assembly"*:

I delight to do Your will, O my God, and Your law is within my heart. I have proclaimed the good news of righteousness in the great assembly; Indeed, I do not restrain my lips, O LORD, You Yourself know. I have not hidden Your righteousness within my heart; I have declared Your faithfulness and Your salvation; I have not concealed Your lovingkindness and Your truth from the great assembly. (Psalm 40:8–10)

Even the king of Ninevah, a former pagan, shared his faith in God with all Ninevah once the Lord got ahold of his life:

Then word came to the king of Nineveh; and he arose from his throne and laid aside his robe, covered himself with sackcloth and sat in ashes. And he caused it to be proclaimed and published throughout Nineveh by the decree of the king and his nobles, saying, Let neither man nor beast, herd nor flock, taste anything; do not let them eat, or drink water. But let man and beast be covered with sackcloth, and cry mightily to God; yes, let every one turn from his evil way and from the violence that is in his hands. (Jonah 3:6–8)

What about those of us who aren't kings and who don't have the opportunity to speak in *"the great assembly"*? Is there still opportunity for us to share our faith, and if so, where should we go? Jesus clarified this issue in Acts 1:8 when He said,

You shall receive power when the Holy Spirit has come upon you; and you shall be witnesses to Me in Jerusalem, and in all Judea and Samaria, and to the end of the earth. (Acts 1:8)

Just as the disciples were called to be witnesses in the areas around them, starting with Jerusalem and moving

outward to the very *"end of the earth,"* Jesus calls us to display this same evangelistic fervor. We are to share the good news of Christ with our immediate circle of friends, and even beyond to those we've never even met!

It's crucial that we heed the call to share our faith; it is not to be taken lightly. The consequences for refusing to share our faith, in fact, can be very serious, according to Jesus:

> *Whatever I tell you in the dark, speak in the light; and what you hear in the ear, preach on the housetops....*
> *Therefore whoever confesses Me before men, him I will also confess before My Father who is in heaven.*
> *But whoever denies Me before men, him I will also deny before My Father who is in heaven.*
> (Matthew 10:27, 32–33)

I hope you're starting to get the picture. No matter where we are or what we do, we are called to share our faith with those around us. This isn't a job just for preachers or missionaries or people called into the full-time ministry. Every single one of us is a full-time Christian, and we are always on duty to give a reason for the hope we have:

> *But sanctify the Lord God in your hearts, and always be ready to give a defense to everyone who asks you a reason for the hope that is in you, with meekness and fear.* (1 Peter 3:15)

Notice how Peter said we are to give our defense *"with meekness and fear."* Does that mean we're supposed to act shy, bashful, afraid, and timid? Not at all! When Peter talked about *"meekness and fear,"* he was talking about gentleness and respect. In other words, when we go to share our faith, we need to avoid an "in your face" attitude. A godly gentleness and respect should be evident to all around us.

Paul had some good advice for how to share faith, as well. Paul was so passionate about sharing his faith, that he would do pretty much anything to get through to someone with the message of Christ. He summed it up nicely in 1 Corinthians 9:19–23:

> *For though I am free from all men, I have made myself a servant to all, that I might win the more; and to the Jews I became as a Jew, that I might win Jews; to those who are under the law, as under the law, that I might win those who are under the law; to those who are without law, as without law (not being without law toward God, but under law toward Christ), that I might win those who are without law; to the weak I became as weak, that I might win the weak. I have become all things to all men, that I might by all means save some. Now this I do for the gospel's sake, that I may be partaker of it with you.*

In other words, Paul wanted to connect with people on a personal level so that they'd be receptive to the gospel message he had to share. We need to do the same in our lives. So often Christians isolate themselves in their stained-glass towers, never coming out to talk to the unsaved world around them. Take time to be friends with non-believers. How else will they ever hear the gospel message?

Share your faith boldly but gently.

Maybe one of your good friends keeps insisting that you join him for a baseball game, for instance. Even though you've never really enjoyed the sport, how about joining him for the next game he invites you to? See it as an opportunity to be *"a servant"* to this friend. As you spend quality time with him, sharing in the things he likes to do, you'll be

able to start doing some "sharing" of your own—sharing that will have amazing, eternal benefits.

Please, my friends, don't be selfish with your faith. Christ has called us to share our faith with others. This is a command we can't afford to ignore.

Day Twenty-Five

Faith must be kept.

F aith is to be kept. Now, when I say "keep the faith," I'm not talking about being all secretive about your faith and "keeping it to yourself." Remember, we are called to leave a legacy of faith for our children and to share our faith with those around us. That doesn't sound like "keeping faith to yourself" to me. On the contrary, when I talk about "keeping the faith," I'm talking about being persistent in your faith. You've got to keep it throughout time. You've got to be faithful in daily living out your faith.

There are many examples in Scripture of people who displayed this kingdom quality of persistence. The apostle Paul is perhaps one of the greatest New Testament examples of this faith-keeping quality. In one of his letters to Timothy, he wrote,

> *For I am already being poured out as a drink offering, and the time of my departure is at hand. I have fought the good fight, I have finished the race, I have kept the faith. Finally, there is laid up for me the crown*

*of righteousness, which the Lord, the righteous Judge,
will give to me on that Day, and not to me only but also
to all who have loved His appearing.*

(2 Timothy 4:6–8)

In the book of Acts, we get to see this faith-keeping persistence of Paul's firsthand. After the apostle Paul had finished a mission's trip in Athens, he journeyed to the city of Corinth, where he spent all his time proclaiming Jesus as the Messiah to both Jews and Gentiles.

Unfortunately, however, the Jews began to oppose Paul and his new take on the Messiah. Their opposition made it increasingly difficult for Paul to continue his ministry to the Jews. Paul decided he had done all he could to try and convince the Jews the truth about the Messiah. From that point on, he decided he would spend the rest of his days targeting the Gentiles with the message of Christ instead of the Jews.

*But when they opposed him and blasphemed, he
shook his garments and said to them, "Your blood be
upon your own heads; I am clean. From now on I will
go to the Gentiles."* (Acts 18:6)

Notice that Paul didn't give up. Faced with a similar situation, many of us would have grown so discouraged that we would have abandoned sharing our faith altogether. "Forget this life of preaching and all the ridicule that comes with it," we might have said. "I'm done sharing. No more faithfulness from me. I'm going on a cruise for the rest of my days—where I can 'faithfully' sleep in every single morning. Now that's a faith I can afford to keep."

Paul, however, didn't do this. He kept the faith. He prepared to shift his focus from the Jews to the Gentiles, but

he kept his focus all the same. Sharing the gospel message of Jesus Christ was his life's desire and aim; nothing would come in the way of that or convince him otherwise.

In the end, God actually called Paul to stay where he was. God changed the hearts of many Jews in that city, and Paul ended up staying in Corinth for a whole year and a half more. Quite a dramatic change for someone who was getting ready to shake his garments of the city's dust and leave for good! It's my opinion that Paul was able to receive this renewed sight from God largely because he was keeping the faith. Had Paul, in frustration, abandoned his ministry altogether, certainly he wouldn't have been part of the great harvest of souls God had in store for him in Corinth!

Of all the qualities that a person could have, I believe that the quality of persistence is one of the greatest. I love to listen to old ministers who have been in ministry for forty, fifty, and sixty or more years. The ones I have a particular attraction to are those ministers whose ministry survived much attack and criti-cism. It inspires me to hear how they persevered although they did not have the support of the people. At times many of them had no financial support at all. Lies and scandal-ous remarks were hurled against many pioneering minis-ters in the first half of the 20th century, yet they survived.

Are you keeping the faith no matter what the cost?

Many of them lived out their fulfilled purpose and call. Obviously it was not because they did not have opposing forces against them. Some of them told me that there were times it seemed as if all of hell came against them, trying every possible tactic to shut them down. In spite of all that,

they lasted. They kept the faith. And because of their persevering spirit not only have they positively influenced and brought healing to thousands and millions of people, but they are now rewarded a crown of life. What a blessing to live the kingdom life. It's an equal blessing to willingly embrace the kingdom quality of persistence.

Far from being something we just "try on for size" or adopt for a day, maybe two, faith is for keeps. When we choose to live by faith, we make long-term, lifelong, never-to-be-broken commitment.

Are you keeping the faith?

DAY TWENTY-SIX

Keeping the faith takes stamina.

I have always liked to watch good boxing matches on television. One of the more pronounced boxing greats that comes to my mind when I think of the sport is the legendary Muhammad Ali. There are at least a dozen books that I can think of that have been written about this man's life and career. Born Cassius Marcellus Clay, Ali stands alone as the greatest boxer of all time.

Out of sixty-one fights, he garnered fifty-six wins and only five loses. Of his wins, thirty-seven were knockouts. He was a 1960 Olympic gold medalist and three-time heavyweight champion of the world. A mouthy contender, one could always hear Ali spewing out some boastful words about himself. He'd say, "I float like a butterfly and sting like a bee." He began to say this mantra so often that it become not only his anthem but also his conviction. He really started to believe that he could not lose.

The first professional fight he lost was in 1971 against Joe Frazier. In this "fight of the century," held at Madison Square Garden, Ali fought to the end. Even after being

knocked down, he managed to stand back up. Although he lost that match in the end, he did not lose his career, his faithful followers, or the boxing legacy that he had worked to establish. Even today he is still recognized as the greatest boxer of all time. His persistence drove him to "stay in the game," even if it meant losing one match to get there. No matter how many times he got knocked down, he would always get back up again.

In the faith realm, this same principle holds true for us as Christians. Keeping the faith takes more than good intentions. It takes determination, hard work, stamina, and endurance. You have to stick with it. When you do get knocked down, you have to realize you haven't been knocked out for good. Instead you get back up, brush yourself off, and keep at it.

Ali's last fight, one against Trevor Berbick, was a loss. Shortly thereafter, Ali announced that he would no longer be fighting professionally. Despite this, I think we'd all agree that Ali didn't "give up" when he ended his career. His determination to light the Olympic torch in Atlanta many years later, despite his devastating battle with Parkinson's disease, was testament to his stick-with-it, fighting spirit. Ali was not a quitter. He was a persister.

> Strong faith takes more than good intentions.

I have a dear minister friend in Connecticut, Pastor Aaron Lewis, whom I've known for nearly a decade. In those first few years after we met, we'd visit each other pretty frequently, and our routine always included a time of fellowshipping and feasting at local restaurants. Aaron was never one to worry about his weight back then. He was a portly man of average height, given to barbecue chicken and beef ribs. In time, our routine became tradition, and every time

Aaron would come visit me in Texas, he'd immediately suggest a dinner at Spring Creek Barbecue so he could order their famous beef ribs and chicken.

Over the years we kept in touch by phone, but our busy schedules prevented us from visiting each other as frequently as we had before. Before I knew it, more than two years had passed since the last time I'd seen my buddy, Aaron.

The next time I saw him, he was about fifty pounds lighter. (Personally, I thought he looked a little too skinny.) As was our custom, we went out to eat, but this time Aaron didn't request his usual Spring Creek Barbecue. I asked him what he wanted to eat, and he told me he wanted, "vegetables, fruits, and pasta." For a minute, I seriously thought he was joking. Wasn't this the same men who used to put away ribs and barbecue chicken like there was no tomorrow?

Aaron went on to tell me how he'd started running marathons and how his diet greatly affected his performance. If he wanted to finish his races, he had to eat a certain way. Some foods, for instance, would give him greater endurance to finish the race. Other foods, however, would seriously sap his stamina and ability to finish the race. So for the sake of his races and overall good health, Aaron avoided certain foods while training his mind to accept new, more healthful foods.

Brother Aaron is concerned about finishing his races, about showing stamina to the end. Because of this, he consciously chooses to eat healthfully every day, a choice that ultimately affects his performance for the best. How about you? Are you feeding your spirit of endurance? It's my prayer that you will show the kind of stick-with-it faith that endures to the end.

DAY TWENTY-SEVEN

Faith must be focused.

*Not that I have already attained, or am already
perfected; but I press on, that I may lay hold
of that for which Christ Jesus has also laid
hold of me. Brethren, I do not count myself to
have apprehended; but one thing I do, forgetting those things which are behind and reaching forward to those things which are ahead,
I press toward the goal for the prize of the
upward call of God in Christ Jesus.*
—Philippians 3:12–14

The apostle Paul had many wonderful attributes. He was scholarly, well-spoken, bold, persistent, and unwavering in the convictions God gave Him. This man of God truly did have a lot of things going for him.

Of all his skills, talents, abilities, and gifts, however, it is my opinion that the greatest gift Paul possessed was his ability to stay focused on the future while simultaneously forgetting the past.

Not that I have already attained,...but I press on.
Philippians 3:12)

Focus is essential for a successful faith walk. In order to grasp new realities, you have to be able to let go of the old ones. Unfortunately, many of us struggle to let go of the past and move on. We dwell on past failures, arguments, hurtful words, and all these things distract and slow us down. Believe it or not, sometimes even the good things of the past can cause problems. If all your energies are spent thinking about that award you got back in 1993, or that successful praise service you lead last fall, or the eloquent prayer you said in Sunday school just a few minutes ago, you're wasting precious energy.

We can't afford to look behind us.

You see, we can't afford to be looking back. We've got pressing on to do! There's a goal ahead, and it should be demanding every ounce of our attention. We've got to let go of the past and focus on the future if we're ever going to have a successful faith walk.

Given the right amount of time, it is my opinion that you will inevitably become whatever you focus on. If you focus on your past, for instance, the chances are high that you'll repeat it. If you focus on the negative words and actions of others, negativity will reproduce itself in your life.

On the other side of the coin, as you begin to focus on good things, positive results will flow through your life. When you focus on a solution instead of a problem, solutions are what you'll get! Even more importantly, when you begin to focus on the person of Christ by studying God's Word and by communicating with Him daily through

Day Twenty-Seven

prayer, your character will become more and more Christ-like with each passing day.

Focus on the Word of God. Focus on the promises of God. Focus on His provision, His glory, and His presence. In time you will receive a harvest of those things because you really do get what you focus on.

DAY TWENTY-EIGHT

Without faith it is impossible to please God.

et me ask you some questions: Do you seek to please God? In other words, is it your desire to bring joy to God's heart? If so, take time to think about how you personally go about doing this. Do you spend time in His Word daily? Do you fellowship and join in corporate worship with other believers? Do you fervently pray for the needs in your own life and the lives of those around you?

I certainly hope you can answer "yes" to each of these questions, for these are all commendable practices that can help you grow in your Christian walk. Scripture reading, Christian fellowship, and daily prayer are all good things. But the fact of the matter is that if you really want to please God, faith is your ticket.

The writer of Hebrews couldn't have been any clearer when he wrote,

But without faith it is impossible to please him: for he that cometh to God must believe that he is, and that he is a rewarder of them that diligently seek him.

(Hebrews 11:6 KJV)

Did you catch that? Without faith it is not just hard or challenging or vexing or difficult to please God—it is impossible! The last time I checked, if something is impossible then that something can't be done. *Merriam-Webster's New Collegiate Dictionary* defines *impossible* like this: "incapable of being or of occurring." There's no way around it. Without faith, we cannot please God. Period. If you want someday to hear, "Well done, My good and faithful servant" (see Matthew 25:21, 23), then you had better start walking in faith.

> If you want to please God, faith is key.

The chapter where we find this verse, Hebrews 11, is frequently referred to as "the faith chapter." It is filled with the accounts of faithful followers from the Old Testament—Abel, Noah, Abraham, Isaac, Jacob, Joseph, Moses. The list goes on and on.

The writer of Hebrews himself said that time and space would not permit him to recount the stories of all the faithful. He wrote,

And what more shall I say? For the time would fail me to tell of Gideon and Barak and Samson and Jephthah, also of David and Samuel and the prophets: who through faith subdued kingdoms, worked righteousness, obtained promises, stopped the mouths of lions, quenched the violence of fire, escaped the edge of the sword, out of weakness were made strong, became

valiant in battle, turned to flight the armies of the aliens. (Hebrews 11:32–34, emphasis added)

"The time would fail me," he wrote. In other words, there are a whole lot of very faithful individuals throughout the history of God's chosen people. Praise God for the wonderful examples He has provided for us!

This sampling of faithful people is pretty impressive. At a glance, it seems the writer of Hebrews is simply trying to emphasize all the great things they did. Look at the many great works performed by these men and women of God:

Abel offered to God a more excellent sacrifice than Cain. (verse 11:4)

Noah...prepared an ark for the saving of his household. (verse 7)

Abraham obeyed when he was called to go out to the place which he would receive as an inheritance. And he went out, not knowing where he was going. (verse 8)

Sarah herself also received strength to conceive seed, and she bore a child when she was past the age. (verse 11)

Abraham, when he was tested, offered up Isaac, and he who had received the promises offered up his only begotten son, of whom it was said, "In Isaac your seed shall be called." (verses 17–18)

Isaac blessed Jacob and Esau concerning things to come. (verse 20)

Jacob, when he was dying, blessed each of the sons of Joseph, and worshiped, leaning on the top of his staff. (verse 21)

Joseph, when he was dying, made mention of the departure of the children of Israel, and gave instructions concerning his bones. (Hebrews 11:22)

Moses, when he became of age, refused to be called the son of Pharaoh's daughter, choosing rather to suffer affliction with the people of God than to enjoy the passing pleasures of sin. (verses 24–25)

[Moses] forsook Egypt, not fearing the wrath of the king....He kept the Passover and the sprinkling of blood. (verses 27–28)

[The Israelites] passed through the Red Sea as by dry land, whereas the Egyptians, attempting to do so, were drowned. (verse 29)

The walls of Jericho fell down after they were encircled for seven days. (verse 30)

The harlot Rahab did not perish with those who did not believe, when she had received the spies with peace. (verse 31)

Gideon and Barak and Samson and Jephthah, also of David and Samuel and the prophets: who through faith subdued kingdoms, worked righteousness, obtained promises, stopped the mouths of lions, quenched the violence of fire, escaped the edge of the sword, out of weakness were made strong, became valiant in battle, turned to flight the armies of the aliens. (verses 32–34)

It would be awfully easy to get the impression from these verses that the writer of Hebrews was concerned with the actions, or works, of these great men and women. Look at all the great things they did! Stopped lions' mouths, quenched fires, escaped death by sword, tore down walls,

prepared to offer their sons for sacrifice—these are great deeds.

There's a key phrase, however, that shows us what's really important: *"By faith."* Almost every single one of these verses starts with the phrase, *"By faith."* That's what was really important in the lives of these men and women. It wasn't their great deeds, although they did have many of them. It was their faith. Their faith was what pleased God, and their faith was what allowed all these great deeds to even happen.

"Without faith it is impossible to please him" (Hebrews 11:6). If you want to please God, faith is the way to do it. All the prayer, Scripture reading, and good deeds in the world won't do any good unless faith is their driving force.

Day Twenty-Nine

Faith chooses to praise and believe in the midst of hardship.

'm sure you've heard the phrase, "fair-weather friends." It's not a complimentary expression. It refers to those people who show loyalty, friendship, and devotion only as long as it benefits them. As soon as a friendship starts to cost them something, though, they flee the scene like there's no tomorrow. They're gone fast! If your friendship benefits them, sure, they'll be happy to stick around. When the rocky times come, however, they're nowhere to be found. It saddens me to say this, but I think we have a lot of "fair-weather faithfuls" in the church today.

Do you know what I'm talking about? I'm talking about the people who are happy to sing God's praises, tell others about Him, and even work to further His kingdom—but only as long as it doesn't cost them anything. As soon as things start to "heat up" and get difficult, they're the first to flee.

This, my friends, is not true faith. In fact, "fair-weather faithfulness" is a contradiction in terms. You're not truly faithful if you're only faithful during the easy times. Genuine faithfulness

chooses to stick with it and still praise God whether life is easy, hard, or somewhere in between. True faithfulness is steady, no matter what.

> Do you have more than just fair-weather faithfulness?

The prophet Habakkuk is a great example of this true faithfulness. Habakkuk, an Old Testament prophet of God, certainly saw some hard times. In the opening verse to his book, Habakkuk called it a *"burden."*

The burden which the prophet Habakkuk saw.

(Habakkuk 1:1)

What exactly did Habakkuk see? The first chapter gives us a pretty good idea:

O Lord, how long shall I cry, and You will not hear? Even cry out to You, "Violence!" and You will not save. Why do You show me iniquity, and cause me to see trouble? For plundering and violence are before me; there is strife, and contention arises. Therefore the law is powerless, and justice never goes forth. For the wicked surround the righteous; therefore perverse judgment proceeds. "Look among the nations and watch; be utterly astounded! For I will work a work in your days which you would not believe, though it were told you. For indeed I am raising up the Chaldeans, a bitter and hasty nation which marches through the breadth of the earth, to possess dwelling places that are not theirs." (verses 2–6)

Habakkuk's *"burden"* was pretty heavy, indeed. He found himself watching as the Lord sent the Chaldeans, who were *"a bitter and hasty nation"* to punish Israel, God's chosen people. The Chaldeans were no ordinary enemy, either. They were heartless, ruthless, and relentless.

They are terrible and dreadful; their judgment and their dignity proceed from themselves. Their horses also are swifter than leopards, and more fierce than evening wolves. Their chargers charge ahead; their cavalry comes from afar; they fly as the eagle that hastens to eat. They all come for violence; their faces are set like the east wind. They gather captives like sand. They scoff at kings, and princes are scorned by them. They deride every stronghold, for they heap up earthen mounds and seize it. Then his mind changes, and he transgresses; he commits offense, ascribing this power to his god. (Habakkuk 1:7–11)

Most importantly, these people were godless! They ascribed their victories to their own false god. They were a people without any true faith whatsoever! How could God let these wicked people take over His chosen nation? Habakkuk wondered:

Are You not from everlasting, O LORD my God, my Holy One? We shall not die. O LORD, You have appointed them for judgment; O Rock, You have marked them for correction. You are of purer eyes than to behold evil, and cannot look on wickedness. Why do You look on those who deal treacherously, and hold Your tongue when the wicked devours a person more righteous than he? Why do You make men like fish of the sea, like creeping things that have no ruler over them? They take up all of them with a hook, they catch them in their net, and gather them in their dragnet. Therefore they rejoice and are glad. Therefore they sacrifice to their net, and burn incense to their dragnet; because by them their share is sumptuous and their food plentiful. Shall they therefore empty their net, and continue to slay nations without pity? (verses 12–17)

From a natural standpoint, Habakkuk probably had every right to abandon his faith at this point, to be nothing more than a "fair-weather faithful." God had abandoned his people, right? Shouldn't Habakkuk have turned away from his faith?

As a person of genuine faith, however, Habakkuk did not operate in the natural. As a faithful follower of God, he was called to live on a higher, supernatural plane. Part of that calling meant remaining faithful when times got tough. And so Habakkuk, in genuine faithfulness, continued to praise His God in the midst of this confusing, trying time:

> *Though the fig tree may not blossom, nor fruit be on the vines; though the labor of the olive may fail, and the fields yield no food; though the flock may be cut off from the fold, and there be no herd in the stalls; yet I will rejoice in the Lord, I will joy in the God of my salvation. The Lord God is my strength; He will make my feet like deer's feet, and He will make me walk on my high hills.*   (Habakkuk 3:17–19)

What an amazing testament of true faith. Habakkuk probably felt anything but worshipful as he saw his fellow countrymen being plundered, ruined, and destroyed by the godless Chaldeans. Through it all, however, Habakkuk chose to still worship. *"Yet I will rejoice in the Lord,"* he said.

What a wonderful word *"yet"* is. That one small, three-letter word says, "Everything around me is crumbling to pieces, and I really don't understand what You're doing, Lord. But in spite of all this, I will worship You." *Yet,* when used this way, needs to be in the vocabulary of every faithful follower. It is a sign of unconditional devotion no matter how trying times may be. It is an expression of genuine, unflinching faith. It is a word that pleases our God.

Have you made the decision to *"yet...rejoice in the Lord,"* no matter what may come?

DAY THIRTY

The faithful are those who refuse to doubt.

In faith there is enough light for those who
want to believe and enough shadows
to blind those who don't.
—Blaise Pascal*

W̶e live in a very doubt-filled society. Expressions
such as "I'll believe it when I see it" and "I highly
doubt it" are pretty commonplace. We can hardly
make it through a single day without encountering at least
one person who expresses "serious doubts" (another popular catchphrase) about one thing or another. Doubt is
rampant and on the loose.

A certain amount of doubt is probably healthy when
it comes to certain things. When a telemarketer calls to
tell you that you can win an all-expense-paid trip to the

* <http://www.quotegarden.com/faith.html> (June 16, 2004)

Bahamas simply by giving them your name, the "doubt-o-meter" in your head will probably go off—as it should. Such an offer sounds too good to be true, and your doubt prompts you to ask questions that will ultimately lead you to a clearer understanding of what exactly is involved in winning this trip. Doubt, like faith, prompts us to action—in this case, action that will help us find out the "real story."

The problem with doubt, however, is that it can quickly start to consume us. What started out as healthy doubt, or simple questioning to find out more, can turn into extreme skepticism and distrustfulness. Such doubt is dangerous and unhealthy, eating away at our ability to trust like a cancer.

There's nowhere this is more true than in the faith realm. We need to be on the lookout for doubt when it comes to the things of God. You see, faith and doubt cannot healthfully coexist. They don't make good roommates. They simply can't get along for any long period of time. Like oil and vinegar, they don't mix.

> Doubt can very quickly consume us.

Is this to say that doubts will never come up in your life? By no means! As a man or woman living on planet Earth, it is inevitable that you will face doubts from time to time. The question is this: What will you do with those doubts?

You're probably familiar with the story of Jesus' disciple Thomas. I'm sure Thomas had moments of great faith, but his one moment of doubt earned him the unfortunate name, "Doubting Thomas."

Now Thomas, called the Twin, one of the twelve, was not with them when Jesus came. The other disciples

therefore said to him, "We have seen the Lord." So he said to them, "Unless I see in His hands the print of the nails, and put my finger into the print of the nails, and put my hand into His side, I will not believe." And after eight days His disciples were again inside, and Thomas with them. Jesus came, the doors being shut, and stood in the midst, and said, "Peace to you!" Then He said to Thomas, "Reach your finger here, and look at My hands; and reach your hand here, and put it into My side. Do not be unbelieving, but believing." And Thomas answered and said to Him, "My Lord and my God!" Jesus said to him, "Thomas, because you have seen Me, you have believed. Blessed are those who have not seen and yet have believed." (John 20:24–29)

Notice how Jesus dealt with Thomas. He didn't yell at him, berate him, or criticize him for his questioning spirit—even though He would have been completely justified in doing so. Instead, Jesus simply relieved Thomas' doubts by letting him see His wounds and then encouraged Thomas to show more faith in the future. *"Blessed are those who have not seen and yet have believed,"* Jesus said, hinting that Thomas—and all of us—should believe whether we have physical proof or not.

One thing we get from this account is a deeper understanding of the extreme love, patience, and grace God extends to those who are His own. He does not want us to doubt. But even when we do, He patiently corrects us and points us back in the right direction.

You see, the initial doubts themselves aren't sinful. It's how you handle the doubts that matters. If you continue to dwell on that doubt and let it control your thinking, you're stepping out of God's will. Such a doubter will not be blessed:

But let him ask in faith, with no doubting, for he who doubts is like a wave of the sea driven and tossed by the wind. (James 1:6)

But if you choose to turn straight to God as soon as the doubts strike, you can rest assured your Lord will take those doubts and transform them into deeper faith.

Shortly after my father died, I went through a season of doubt when I struggled greatly with my Christian faith. "How could God have allowed my father to pass away at what appeared to be the peak of his ministry?" I wondered. Doubt assailed me on every side.

This time of doubt was one of the most difficult seasons of my life. And when I established my own ministry a few years down the road, the doubt struck again. I had held my father in such high esteem that I often doubted my own calling. In my doubt, however, I did not turn away. Instead, these doubts drove me to my knees. As I struggled with my doubts, I turned to Christ and laid them at His feet.

Doubts are inevitable, but letting them rule our lives is not. As Christians, we are to walk in faith. When doubts come, refuse and then choose! Refuse to listen to the doubts, and then choose to operate by faith instead. As you turn to Christ with your doubts, you'll see Him drive them away, one by one. In their place, you'll have a renewed and deeper faith.

DAY THIRTY-ONE

Faith leads to faithfulness.

When a person walks in godly faith, faithfulness follows close behind—or at least it should.

By *faithfulness*, I mean loyalty, fidelity, devotion, allegiance. If you're being faithful in the sense of "faith-full," that is, having true faith in God, then the quality of loyalty and devotion—or faithfulness—should be present in your life, as well.

One of the greatest biblical examples of faithfulness is of a man we don't frequently discuss in our Sunday morning sermons, Wednesday night Bible studies, or yearly Vacation Bible School lessons. He was a man of great faith, but he often gets more of a footnote in our thoughts than a place of prominence. It's my opinion, though, that this lesser-known, lesser-mentioned man of God lived out a life of great faith.

When many people think of "great faith," they picture huge acts of courage, dramatic anointings, and miraculous occurrences. Many men and women of great faith, however, are more ordinary than this. They may not have a donkey's

jawbone like Samson, five smooth stones like David, a mantle like Elijah, or an ark like Noah—but they're still men and women of great faith. Faith doesn't always take center stage; sometimes it's busy taking care of things off in the wings—but its role there is just as important as its role under the spotlight.

At any rate, the man of faith I'd like to discuss was definitely an "in-the-wings" type of person. He was by no means in the limelight. In fact, he lived in the shadows of King David's castle. The man I'm talking about is Uriah.

Faith doesn't always take center stage.

Uriah was a soldier in king David's army. He was also husband to a woman David coveted—and actually committed adultery with. Yes, David, the great patriarch of faith—the man after God's own heart!—was the villain in this story. Here's what happened:

> *In the spring of the year, at the time when kings go out to battle, that David sent Joab and his servants with him, and all Israel; and they destroyed the people of Ammon and besieged Rabbah. But David remained at Jerusalem. Then it happened one evening that David arose from his bed and walked on the roof of the king's house. And from the roof he saw a woman bathing, and the woman was very beautiful to behold. So David sent and inquired about the woman. And someone said, "Is this not Bathsheba, the daughter of Eliam, the wife of Uriah the Hittite?" Then David sent messengers, and took her; and she came to him, and he lay with her, for she was cleansed from her impurity; and she returned to her house. And the woman conceived; so she sent and told David, and said, "I am with child."* (2 Samuel 11:1–5)

Now the number one problem was that David should have been at the battleground giving orders to his troops, but he was home instead. Remember, the Scripture says it was *"the spring of the year,...the time when kings go out to battle,"* yet David stayed home and sent Joab out to do his job. That's another message for another time, but just remember this important point: When you're not where you're supposed to be, you're setting yourself up for trouble. Had David been out on the field, he never would have seen Bathsheba and been tempted as he was. But anyway, on to Uriah.

When David found out Bathsheba was pregnant, he knew he had to think fast. Knowing her pregnancy could have huge political implications for him, or lead to accusations of adultery for her, David's heart began to fill with fear. He felt a cover-up was the only solution and quickly set to work devising what he thought was a perfect, foolproof plan.

> *Then David sent to Joab, saying, "Send me Uriah the Hittite." And Joab sent Uriah to David. When Uriah had come to him, David asked how Joab was doing, and how the people were doing, and how the war prospered. And David said to Uriah, "Go down to your house and wash your feet." So Uriah departed from the king's house, and a gift of food from the king followed him.* (2 Samuel 11:6–8)

David hoped to encourage an intimate evening between Bathsheba and her husband. Why? So that she would appear to be pregnant by her husband. Unfortunately for David, things didn't work according to plan.

> *But Uriah slept at the door of the king's house with all the servants of his lord, and did not go down to his*

house. So when they told David, saying, "Uriah did not go down to his house," David said to Uriah, "Did you not come from a journey? Why did you not go down to your house?" And Uriah said to David, "The ark and Israel and Judah are dwelling in tents, and my lord Joab and the servants of my lord are encamped in the open fields. Shall I then go to my house to eat and drink, and to lie with my wife? As you live, and as your soul lives, I will not do this thing." Then David said to Uriah, "Wait here today also, and tomorrow I will let you depart." So Uriah remained in Jerusalem that day and the next. Now when David called him, he ate and drank before him; and he made him drunk. And at evening he went out to lie on his bed with the servants of his lord, but he did not go down to his house.

(2 Samuel 9–13)

This is where Uriah's faithfulness comes in. His great faith in the King of all creation showed itself through obedience and devotion to his earthly king, King David. As he said to David,

The ark and Israel and Judah are dwelling in tents, and my lord Joab and the servants of my lord are encamped in the open fields. Shall I then go to my house to eat and drink, and to lie with my wife? As you live, and as your soul lives, I will not do this thing.

No doubt Uriah was tired, hungry, and wanting to spend time with his wife. He'd just been out fighting a war, for goodness sake! Surely he longed for the comforts of home. But he could not, in right conscience, indulge himself when his fellow soldiers, his nation, his king, and his God needed him to remain faithful to the cause he had signed up for. And so he chose to sleep outside instead, never setting foot inside his own home.

Day Thirty-One

You probably know how the story ends. David, angered by Uriah's unexpected faithfulness, ended up sending him to the front lines so he would be killed. David's scheme worked, Uriah was killed, and the king took Bathsheba as his wife shortly thereafter, making for a not-so-happy ending to a sad but true story of sin. And yet God did not abandon David for his sinfulness. Sure, God rebuked David, and the royal couple definitely had their share of trials because of this sin. But God, in His mercy, still fellowshipped with David—and even still allowed David to be part of Christ's bloodline. What an amazing and gracious God we serve to forgive wretched sinners like us!

To return to Uriah, the lesson we learn from his story is this: Faith isn't always shown in great feats of strength. Sometimes it's quiet and unassuming—choosing to sleep outside, cold and hungry, when you'd rather be home with your wife, eating a home-cooked meal. No matter how quiet faith is, though, it's still great in God's eyes. Faithfulness is faithfulness, whether the whole world sees it or not. Are you being faithful, committed, and loyal, even when there's no one watching? I challenge you to examine your life and answer that question with all honesty and prayerfulness. And remember, if you're lacking in faith, don't despair. Turn to your heavenly Father, for He is our gracious Provider, eager to equip us with all we need to further glorify Him.

> Sometimes faith is quiet and unassuming.

Ask, and it will be given to you; seek, and you will find; knock, and it will be opened to you. For everyone who asks receives, and he who seeks finds, and to him who knocks it will be opened. (Matthew 7:7–8)

DAY THIRTY-TWO

Faith is constantly under attack by the Adversary.

The great sixteenth-century author, philosopher, scientist, inventor, diplomat, and philanthropist Benjamin Franklin is credited with penning the now familiar saying, "In this world nothing can be said to be certain, except death and taxes."*

While I think we can all agree that there is more to be certain about in life than just death and taxes, this quote is a humorous reminder that no matter how hard we try to avoid taxes, it can't be done. Taxes are as inevitable as death.

In the Christian life, the same holds true for spiritual attack. Plain and simple, it is unavoidable. Satan is none to happy about us serving God, and he will pull out all the stops to try and make us stumble. He is relentless.

---

* Benjamin Franklin, 1789 letter to Jean-Baptiste Leroy, Wikiquote, 18 June 2004. <http://quote.wikipedia.org/wiki/Benjamin_Franklin> (7 June 2004)

Be sober, be vigilant; because your adversary the devil walks about like a roaring lion, seeking whom he may devour. Resist him, steadfast in the faith, knowing that the same sufferings are experienced by your brotherhood in the world. (1 Peter 5:8–9)

Maybe you've seen this in your own life. Perhaps things were going pretty smoothly—good health, sound finances, steady job, rewarding relationships. As soon as you made that decision to step out and grow in your faith, however, you found yourself struggling on practically every front. Suddenly, you're tired all the time and it's a battle to get out of bed. Your car, which has always been reliable, starts making strange noises and funny smells—which the garage says will cost $1500 to fix! At work, you start wondering if the new employee is being trained to take over your position. And your marriage—well, the two of you have been fighting over the silliest little things more than ever before!

While many of life's struggles are simply consequences of the fallen, sinful world we live in, sometimes trials such as these are direct attacks from Satan. Remember, he is a prowling, *"roaring lion, seeking whom he may devour."* He definitely has an agenda, and that agenda includes bringing us down!

My father's ministry garnered more criticism and attack than anyone's ministry I know of today. The Adversary was definitely out to get him. Yet through it all, he remained faithful to his calling and dedicated to serving God, whatever the cost. Wherever God told him to go, my father was there, setting up gospel tents to preach salvation and healing in Jesus' name. He was truly a man of reckless faith, a bold and fearless follower of God.

In other words, he was exactly the kind of man the Devil would have liked to trip up. And Satan certainly

did try! In February of 1956, my father preached a series of revival services in Miami, Florida, where many people where miraculously healed by the power of God. These supernatural healings were so amazing that news quickly spread to people in the community. Of course the Devil hated what was happening, and he made it his job to stop it. To my dad's surprise, the police arrested him.

The police accused my father of "practicing medicine without a license." Of course the allegations were totally untrue. My father never administered medication to the people he prayed for. I know that their healings were completely from the hand of God. Yet, the wicked powers and spirits on that day knew very well that my father's faith in Jesus would soon "infect" everyone with the powerful message of Jesus Christ. They felt they were left with no choice but to shut his meetings down. And shut him down they did by bringing false, trumped-up charges against him.

> Our Foe is relentless, but we must be more so.

Fortunately they didn't shut him down for good. After his arrest, my dad called friends all across the country to come and testify on his behalf. A lot of preachers wouldn't come, fearful of how such exposure might adversely affect their ministries. Many others, however, did come to testify on my father's behalf, including Gordon Lindsay, founder of Christ for the Nations Institute, and healing evangelist Raymond Richey. As always, God prevailed, and my father found favor with the judge. He was released, and the case was dismissed.

What I see in this story is the relentlessness of our Foe. He wants to stop us, and he'll try any means to do so, no matter how extreme! Our job when faced with such attacks is to stand strong, keep preaching, hold to the faith, and never surrender! Remember the passage from 1 Peter 5:

Be sober, be vigilant; because your adversary the devil walks about like a roaring lion, seeking whom he may devour. Resist him, steadfast in the faith, knowing that the same sufferings are experienced by your brotherhood in the world. (verses 8–9)

How did Peter say we should respond to the Adversary's attacks? We are to *"resist him"* while remaining *"steadfast in the faith."* We can do this because we know that the Adversary, no matter how powerful he might seem, is a defeated foe. Because of Christ's work on the cross, Satan has already been conquered—and he will be bound forever when Christ comes again to take us home!

So when this corruptible has put on incorruption, and this mortal has put on immortality, then shall be brought to pass the saying that is written: "Death is swallowed up in victory." "O Death, where is your sting? O Hades, where is your victory?" The sting of death is sin, and the strength of sin is the law. But thanks be to God, who gives us the victory through our Lord Jesus Christ. (1 Corinthians 15:54–57)

Having disarmed principalities and powers, He made a public spectacle of them, triumphing over them in it. (Colossians 2:15)

And war broke out in heaven: Michael and his angels fought with the dragon; and the dragon and his angels fought, but they did not prevail, nor was a place found for them in heaven any longer. So the great dragon was cast out, that serpent of old, called the Devil and Satan, who deceives the whole world; he was cast to the earth, and his angels were cast out with him. Then I heard a loud voice saying in heaven, "Now salvation, and strength, and the kingdom of our God, and the

Day Thirty-Two

power of His Christ have come, for the accuser of our brethren, who accused them before our God day and night, has been cast down. (Revelation 12:7–10)

Praise be to God that our Enemy is defeated! Attacks on our faith may be a guaranteed fact—but so is our ultimate victory in Jesus Christ our Lord. Hallelujah!

DAY THIRTY-THREE

Faith is about God, not us.

[Abraham] *contrary to hope, in hope believed, so that
he became the father of many nations, according to
what was spoken, "So shall your descendants be."
And not being weak in faith, he did not consider his
own body, already dead (since he was about a hundred years old), and the deadness of Sarah's womb.
He did not waver at the promise of God through
unbelief, but was strengthened in faith, giving glory
to God, and being fully convinced that what He had
promised He was also able to perform.*
—Romans 4:18–21

If I were to ask you, "Why is it important to have faith?"
how would you respond? Take a second right now and
reflect on that question. I'm asking you now, Why do
you think it is important to have faith?

Perhaps some of the following capture your reasons for
having faith:

- Without faith, I feel like a ship tossed at sea.
- Faith gives me direction and purpose in life.
- When I'm walking in faith, I feel more at peace.

While it's true that faith gives us stability, direction, purpose, and peace, I'd like to suggest that there's an even greater reason for having faith. Sure we reap immeasurable benefits from having faith, but what should be the ultimate goal? You got it: glorifying God.

> **All creation exists to glorify God.**

The Bible is filled with reminders that *all* of creation—from the stars in the sky to the pebbles at our feet, from the birds of the air to the ants on the ground, from the most faithful follower of Christ to the one who actually scorns Him—exists for the purpose of glorifying God.

The heavens declare the glory of God; and the firmament shows His handiwork. Day unto day utters speech, and night unto night reveals knowledge. There is no speech nor language where their voice is not heard. (Psalm 19:1–3)

Because of this, we are to make it our goal to glorify Him in all that we do:

For you were bought at a price; therefore glorify God in your body and in your spirit, which are God's.
(1 Corinthians 6:20)

Therefore, whether you eat or drink, or whatever you do, do all to the glory of God. (1 Corinthians 10:31)

This knowledge—that we are doing all things for His glory—makes even the most trying of circumstances able to be not just *endured* but actually *embraced*:

And since we have the same spirit of faith, according to what is written, "I believed and therefore I spoke," we also believe and therefore speak, knowing that He who raised up the Lord Jesus will also raise us up with Jesus, and will present us with you. For all things are for your sakes, that grace, having spread through the many, may cause thanksgiving to abound to the glory of God.

(2 Corinthians 4:13–15)

Yet if anyone suffers as a Christian, let him not be ashamed, but let him glorify God in this matter. (1 Peter 4:16)

Do you see how important it is to glorify God? Time and time again, the Scriptures return to this message. All things exist for the glory of God, to satisfy Him and bring Him praise. And this truth applies to faith, as well.

Do you remember the story of Abraham? Or perhaps I should say "stories," for the book of Genesis is filled with accounts of his amazing faith. That man had powerful faith. At one point God told Abraham to kill his only son—the son through whom God was supposed to be blessing Abraham with many descendants! Abraham followed in obedience, never questioning God. Now that's faith! Fortunately for Abraham, God intervened and supplied another sacrifice, a ram, right as Abraham was about to drive the knife into his son. Talk about faith's rewards being right on time! (You can read the entire account, including God's promise to bless Abraham through Isaac, in Genesis 17; 22:1–18.)

At any rate, we know that Abraham's faithfulness, both in this instance and throughout his life, were pleasing and glorifying to God. How do we know this? Because Scripture tells us. In the New Testament, Paul wrote,

And not being weak in faith, he did not consider his own body, already dead (since he was about a hundred years old), and the deadness of Sarah's womb.

He did not waver at the promise of God through unbe-
lief, but was strengthened in faith, giving glory to God,
and being fully convinced that what He had promised
He was also able to perform.   (Romans 4:19–21)

Did you catch that? As Abraham was *"strengthened in*
faith," he gave *"glory to God."* Abraham's faith pleased God
and was a sweet aroma to Him, and our faith can be the
same!

How, exactly, does our faith please God and bring glory
to His name? I'm glad you asked. You see, our faith glorifies
God because it provides an avenue for Him to prove His
God-ness and goodness. When we walk in faith, we show
that we trust Him. And when we show that we trust Him,
we proclaim to the unbelieving world around us that our
God is mighty and able to do all things!

I like the way contemporary pastor and author John
Piper explained it in one of his Sunday morning sermons.
He addressed it to the children in the congregation, but I
think it's a good explanation that's easy for all of us—adult
and children alike—to understand.

> Your daddy is standing in a swimming pool out a little
> bit from the edge. You are, let's say, three years old
> and standing on the edge of the pool. Daddy holds out
> his arms to you and says, "Jump, I'll catch you. I prom-
> ise." Now, how do you make your daddy look good at
> that moment? Answer: Trust him and jump. Have faith
> in him and jump. That makes him look strong and
> wise and loving. But if you won't jump, if you shake
> your head and run away from the edge, you make your
> daddy look bad. It looks like you are saying, "He can't
> catch me" or "He won't catch me" or "It's not a good

Day Thirty-Three

idea to do what he tells me to do." And all three of those make your dad look bad.

But you don't want to make God look bad. So you trust Him. Then you make Him look good—which He really is. And that is what we mean when we say, "Faith glorifies God" or "Faith gives God glory." It makes Him look as good as He really is.*

Are you walking in faith, ready to jump whenever God says? If so, why? Do you have His glory as your heart's interest, or are you solely concerned with the benefits you'll get out of it? I challenge you to start living in faith not for your own glory, but for God's. The wonderful irony is that the more you shift your focus from what faith can do for you to how your faith glorifies God, the more you'll probably find yourself being blessed because of it. What a good God we serve!

---

* John Piper, © Desiring God Ministries, www.desiringGOD.org.
<http://www.desiringgod.org/library/sermons/99/092699.html>
(15 June 2004)

DAY THIRTY-FOUR

Faith is not something we can judge in others.

Judge not, that you be not judged. For with what judgment you judge, you will be judged; and with the measure you use, it will be measured back to you.
—Matthew 7:1–2

This is perhaps one of the most difficult commandments for many Christians to obey. I don't care where you live, where you go to church, what denomination you're in, or who your pastor is. It seems that church people everywhere are prone being judgmental. Somehow we think we have the capacity—and the calling—to judge how much faith others have and then promptly proclaim our findings to anyone and everyone.

Now I know Jesus said, *"Therefore by their fruits you will know them"* (Matthew 7:20). There's nothing wrong with looking for fruit in a person's life to determine if that person is connected to the Vine or not. After all, Jesus

told us that this is how we would know who belonged to Him and who didn't. The problems start, however, when we appoint ourselves as not just the "fruit inspectors" but the official "pruners," as well. I'm talking about the Christians who decide it's their duty to lecture every unfruitful branch—or even tell those branches that they don't belong and might as well just leave the church.

This is judgment at its worst! The last time I checked, God was the one in charge of pruning and branch removal. As Jesus said, *"I am the true vine, and My Father is the vinedresser. Every branch in Me that does not bear fruit **He takes away**; and every branch that bears fruit **He prunes**, that it may bear more fruit"* (John 15:1–2). Since when are we in charge of deciding which branches should stay and which should go? That's God's job!

Thank goodness He's the one in charge of pruning. You see, God alone has the right to judge because God alone upholds the standards. Why should we be allowed to judge others for their slipups, shortcomings, or even sins, when we ourselves are guilty of the exact same things—or even worse! Jesus said it like this:

> And why do you look at the speck in your brother's eye, but do not consider the plank in your own eye? Or how can you say to your brother, "Let me remove the speck from your eye"; and look, a plank is in your own eye? Hypocrite! First remove the plank from your own eye, and then you will see clearly to remove the speck from your brother's eye. (Matthew 7:3–5)

Jesus told us here that once we've dealt with our own lack of fruit—or abundance of rotten fruit, as the case may be—then and only then can we approach others about the problems we see in their lives. Even this, however, is not

to be done with a judgmental, condescending attitude. On the contrary, we are to approach those who are either weak in faith or presently stumbling in the faith with gentleness and love.

> *Brethren, if a man is overtaken in any trespass, you who are spiritual restore such a one in a spirit of gentleness, considering yourself lest you also be tempted.*
> (Galatians 6:1)

It's not that we should never confront a brother or sister who's walking in sin. Remember, we *are* responsible for holding each accountable. Holding someone accountable, however, does not mean appointing yourself Supreme Court Justice of his or her life. Don't forget the *"spirit of gentleness"*!

In addition to all of this is the important fact that God sees final outcomes long before we ever do. Sometimes, while we're busy casting judgment on others, God's busy looking ahead to the wonderful, God-glorifying future He has planned for those individuals. He knows how things are going to turn out. It could very well be that the person you're wasting your time judging and complaining about is the next Billy Graham, or C. H. Spurgeon, or D. L. Moody; and that

God's in charge of pruning, not us.

God, in His sovereignty, is getting ready to use the present season of sinfulness and backsliding in that person's life for ultimate good, to bring that individual into deeper relationship with Him in the long run. You have no idea what God has in the works! Why waste your energy heartlessly judging and condemning when it's all in God's hands?

Suppose your automobile engine needed to be overhauled so you took your car to the neighborhood mechanic

for repairs. If your mechanic allowed you to visit the garage while he was working on your car, you might be somewhat discouraged and puzzled to see your engine's parts scattered all over the garage floor. "What a mess!" you might think. "Is he fixing my engine or actually breaking it more?" The mechanic, however, would see things in a totally different light. He'd see a project well on its way to being done, a good-as-new engine nearly completed.

That's how God views us. Remember, we are all works in progress. Not a single one of us has attained perfection yet. The good news is that, while we may look like a mess to everyone around us right now, we won't look that way forever. We have an eternal home waiting, a home where sin and imperfection cannot dwell. In that glorious place, there will be *"no more death, nor sorrow, nor crying"* (Revelation 21:4)—and, I dare say, no more hypocritical judging. In the meantime, let's allow God to replace our judgmental spirits with spirits of gentleness and of love.

DAY THIRTY-FIVE

Faith is NOT the absence of fear.

Awhole lot of people falsely teach that faith is the absence of fear. "If you have faith," they say, "you can face anything. Nothing will scare you." Well, friends, I'm here to tell you that faith is *not* simply the absence of fear. If you were scared of heights before you came to faith, you're probably going to have that same fear after you become a Christian. Likewise, just because you accept Christ doesn't mean your fear of spiders is going to suddenly disappear. Fear and faith are *not* mutually exclusive.

However, faith does greatly affect how we respond to fear. Specifically, faith is not the *absence* of fear but rather the *courage* to face and ultimately overcome our fears. The person of faith might still feel fearful at times, but he's also equipped with the tools to tackle his fears. He can look fear straight in the face and say, "You know what? You're nothing next to my God. With God by my side, I don't have to be afraid of you!"

Do you remember the story of the twelve spies who brought back a report on the Promised Land? The Israelites, after wandering through the desert for many years under

Moses' leadership, finally arrived at Canaan's borders. The Promised Land was in sight. God told Moses to send a group of twelve to explore the land before everyone entered, so Moses gathered together twelve spies, one from each tribe, and sent them to check out Canaan.

> *Then Moses sent them to spy out the land of Canaan, and said to them, "Go up this way into the South, and go up to the mountains, and see what the land is like: whether the people who dwell in it are strong or weak, few or many; whether the land they dwell in is good or bad; whether the cities they inhabit are like camps or strongholds; whether the land is rich or poor; and whether there are forests there or not. Be of good courage. And bring some of the fruit of the land."*
>
> (Numbers 13:17–20)

The twelve men did as they were commanded, exploring deep into the interior of Canaan. Forty days later, they returned—with huge clusters of fruit to show how plentiful and rich this land of milk and honey really was!

> *Then they came to the Valley of Eshcol, and there cut down a branch with one cluster of grapes; they carried it between two of them on a pole. They also brought some of the pomegranates and figs. The place was called the Valley of Eshcol, because of the cluster which the men of Israel cut down there. And they returned from spying out the land after forty days....Then they told [Moses], and said: "We went to the land where you sent us. It truly flows with milk and honey, and this is its fruit."*
>
> (verses 23–25, 27)

What joy these men must have been feeling. After forty years of wandering, they were finally reaching the Promised Land—and it was even more bountiful than they had imagined. Unfortunately, though, not everyone in the group

was overjoyed. Some of the spies were downright scared of the men who lived in Canaan. They told Moses,

> *"The people who dwell in the land are strong; the cities are fortified and very large; moreover we saw the descendants of Anak there. The Amalekites dwell in the land of the South; the Hittites, the Jebusites, and the Amorites dwell in the mountains; and the Canaanites dwell by the sea and along the banks of the Jordan.... We are not able to go up against the people, for they are stronger than we." And they gave the children of Israel a bad report of the land which they had spied out, saying, "The land through which we have gone as spies is a land that devours its inhabitants, and all the people whom we saw in it are men of great stature. There we saw the giants (the descendants of Anak came from the giants); and we were like grasshoppers in our own sight, and so we were in their sight."*
>   (Numbers 13:28–29, 31–33)

Caleb interrupted, reminding his fellow spies that God was big enough to handle these giants. *"Let us go up at once and take possession,"* he said, *"for we are well able to overcome it"* (verse 30). His words, however, were to no avail. The stubborn Israelites continued weeping and worrying about the Canaanites:

> *So all the congregation lifted up their voices and cried, and the people wept that night. And all the children of Israel complained against Moses and Aaron, and the whole congregation said to them, "If only we had died in the land of Egypt! Or if only we had died in this wilderness!"*   (Numbers 14:1–2)

Why the difference in opinions? Why was Caleb eager to take the land while most of the other spies were eager to

flee? Did Caleb not see the giants? Or perhaps he just had a spine of steel—a fearless, valiant warrior.

I'd like to suggest that neither of these explains Caleb's apparent lack of fear. As we see a few verses later, Caleb definitely saw the same giants. So did Joshua, another spy who apparently wasn't afraid of the giants. Their response to the people, however, shows that they weren't blind or dumb. They knew the Canaanites were a scary crew—but they also knew their God was mightier!

> **Faith doesn't ignore fear, it just refuses to let it grow.**

But Joshua the son of Nun and Caleb the son of Jephunneh, who were among those who had spied out the land, tore their clothes; and they spoke to all the congregation of the children of Israel, saying: "The land we passed through to spy out is an exceedingly good land. If the LORD delights in us, then He will bring us into this land and give it to us, 'a land which flows with milk and honey.' Only do not rebel against the LORD, nor fear the people of the land, for they are our bread; their protection has departed from them, and the LORD is with us. Do not fear them."

(Numbers 14:6–9)

Joshua and Caleb didn't ignore the reality around them. They saw the same giants as the other ten spies. It's very likely they felt fear in the pit of their stomachs just like the others when they first came face-to-face with the giants of Canaan. What Joshua and Caleb *didn't* do, though, was allow seeds of fear to grow within them. They acknowledged their fear and then they returned their thoughts to the promises of God. "If the Lord wants to give us this land," they said, "then He certainly will. He is more than able!"

Day Thirty-Five

This is the approach we need to take when find our-selves facing potentially frightening situations. When you're up against a giant, a fearful foe, do you immediately forget your wonder-working God? Or do you turn your thoughts to Him, squashing all fears in the process? When we dwell and reflect upon our God and His promises, it's hard for the fear to stay around. Remember,

> *He Himself has said, "I will never leave you nor for-sake you."*   (Hebrews 13:5)

When I was diagnosed with colon cancer and told I was going to die, I have to admit that I was a bit concerned. I did not allow that seed of fear to grow within me, however. Instead I immediately turned to God's Word and began my own "replacement therapy." Whenever worries, fearful-ness, or anxious thoughts crept into my heart, I'd *replace* them with promises from God's Word. What a mighty work that did! It wasn't that I was fearless—it was that God, in His graciousness, transformed my fears into an even stron-ger faith.

DAY THIRTY-SIX

Faith people speak a totally different language.

For those who say such things declare plainly that they
seek a homeland....But now they desire a better, that is,
a heavenly country. Therefore God is not ashamed to be
called their God, for He has prepared a city for them.
—Hebrews 11:14, 16

As people of faith, we have a homeland waiting for us, a *"better,...heavenly country."* Now, no country is complete without a language, or at least a dialect, of its own. The people of France speak French, the people of Spain speak Spanish, and the people of Germany speak German. Sure, there are other countries where these same languages are spoken; most of the people in Peru, Mexico, Honduras, and Chile, for instance, all speak Spanish, but each of these nations also has its own variation, its own dialect, of Spanish. With nationhood comes an official language. And as citizens of heaven, we are called to speak the language of our homeland—the language of faith.

Before we can speak a language, we have to learn it. So, what does the language of faith sound like? Well, one thing is for sure: There are certain sayings that simply cannot be translated into the language of faith. You'll never find the expression, "It can't be done," for instance, in faith's lexicon, and there's no translation for, "I'll never get out of this mess." Instead, the person of faith realizes, *"I can do all things through Christ who strengthens me"* (Philippians 4:13), and that's the truth he speaks. Likewise, "Why did this have to happen to me?" isn't in faith's vocabulary, either. The closest translation is, *"We know that all things work together for good to those who love God, to those who are the called according to His purpose"* (Romans 8:28).

> Faith realizes the power of words.

The strong in faith speak differently from almost everyone else around them. While the poor in faith speak despairingly whenever life deals unexpected blows, the rich in faith recognize *all* experiences as opportunities for God to send His blessings. When a nonbeliever loses his job, for instance, the first thing out of his mouth might be, "I'm doomed! How am I ever going to pay off my mortgage, my school loans, *and* my car payments? Why did this have to happen? How am I going to make it?"

The person of strong faith, however, takes what ends up being a more optimistic approach. His reaction might be something more like this: "Well, I lost my job, and that doesn't exactly thrill me. But you know what? I realize that I am in Your hands, God, and that You will work out this situation however You see fit. I *know* that You will provide for my needs, because You promised Your children that You would. If You took care of the lilies, I know You'll take care of me. Thank You, Lord! I'm excited to see what You have in store!"

Day Thirty-Six

As faith-filled people, it is crucial that we watch our words. The Bible is full of teachings on the power of the tongue. Here are just a few:

The tongue of the righteous is choice silver; the heart of the wicked is worth little. (Proverbs 10:20)

There is one who speaks like the piercings of a sword, but the tongue of the wise promotes health. The truthful lip shall be established forever, but a lying tongue is but for a moment. (Proverbs 12:18–19)

The tongue of the wise uses knowledge rightly, but the mouth of fools pours forth foolishness....A wholesome tongue is a tree of life, But perverseness in it breaks the spirit. (Proverbs 15:2, 4)

By long forbearance a ruler is persuaded, and a gentle tongue breaks a bone. (Proverbs 25:15)

Not what goes into the mouth defiles a man; but what comes out of the mouth, this defiles a man. (Matthew 15:11)

If anyone among you thinks he is religious, and does not bridle his tongue but deceives his own heart, this one's religion is useless. (James 1:26)

He who would love life and see good days, let him refrain his tongue from evil, and his lips from speaking deceit. (1 Peter 3:10)

Why is it so important to be careful of what we say? Why does God place such emphasis on the taming of our tongues? They say actions speak louder than words—so it really doesn't matter what we say. Right?

Wrong.

As James wrote in his epistle, the tongue is powerful—and as untamable as fire!

> *Even so the tongue is a little member and boasts great things. See how great a forest a little fire kindles! And the tongue is a fire, a world of iniquity. The tongue is so set among our members that it defiles the whole body, and sets on fire the course of nature; and it is set on fire by hell. For every kind of beast and bird, of reptile and creature of the sea, is tamed and has been tamed by mankind. But no man can tame the tongue. It is an unruly evil, full of deadly poison.* (James 3:5–8)

Proverbs 6:2 puts it another way: *"You are snared by the words of your mouth; you are taken by the words of your mouth."*

A snare is nothing more than a small trap used for catching animals. So, to put it another way, our words can trap us, holding us captive to whatever we speak. Our tongues are so hard to tame and control—and yet they end up controlling *us* so easily! We see this time and time again in the lives of those who only know the negative. They grow up hearing the words, "You'll never amount to anything," repeated over and over again until they start saying these words themselves. As they repeat these words, they internalize them and, eventually, start to believe them. Some might call it "self-fulfilling prophecy." The Bible calls it "being snared."

I don't know about you, but I'd rather not be held captive by my words. As a *"bondservant of Christ"* (Galatians 1:10), I'm captive to Christ and Christ alone! I will not let my mouth be my master. Instead, I will tame it and use it to bring glory to the King of Kings, the Lord of Lords, and the great Master of all creation. Praise God from whom all blessings flow!

Day Thirty-Seven

Faith's fruits are always right on time.

There's a funny story about a factory manager whose employees kept returning late from their lunch breaks. Whenever the whistle blew to call the men back to work, only a few were at their machines. Finally the manager realized he needed to do something about it, so he put a sign by the company suggestion box offering a cash award to whoever best answered the question, "What can we do to make sure every man is inside the factory when the whistle blows?" Many of the employees submitted suggestions, and the one that solved the problem was selected as the winner. The suggestion that the manager *really* liked best, however, was one he couldn't use. It read, "Let the last man in blow the whistle."*

Just like this manager, we've all had to deal with things being less than timely. Perhaps your paycheck came late in the mail. Maybe the bus arrived ten minutes later than it was supposed to. Or perhaps you were kept in the doctor's

---

* <http://www.christianglobe.com/Illustrations/theDetails.asp?which One=1&whichFile=late> (15 June 2004)

office waiting room an hour longer than you had antici-pated. Or maybe you've been the one to make others wait. From traffic jams and road construction to unexpected phone calls and last-minute "emergencies" on our way out the door, life is full of things that make us late. For some people, being late is pretty much a way of life.

Sometimes delinquency doesn't matter. If you're late for work because of a traffic jam caused by an accident, your boss will more than likely understand and not lecture you too much. Likewise, that extra hour in the doctor's office usually doesn't throw off your whole life's plans. Other times, however, delin-quency can be hard to swallow—if not downright painful.

> Our Lord and Savior is never late.

The famous Greek playwright Euripedes is attributed with saying, "I hate it in friends when they come too late to help."* Perhaps you can relate. Have you been on the receiving end of too-late sympathies or offers to help? It's not the easiest thing to take.

Fortunately, we have one friend who has never been, never is, and never will be late. This is no ordinary friend. Do you know who I'm talking about? I'm talking about Jesus Christ. As the old hymn says, "What a Friend We Have in Jesus!" What a friend indeed! He is always on time.

If you want to see some amazing examples of what it means to be on time, just take a look at the created order around you. Salmon, robins, and maple trees don't own clocks or calendars, but every year they know exactly when

---

* Euripides, Greek playwright, c. 480–406 BC. <http://en.thinkexist. com/search/searchquotation.asp?search=late&page=4> (15 June 2004)

to swim upstream, migrate to the south, and start produc-ing leaves, respectively. Why? Because the God who cre-ated them is an on time God.

If you ever have a chance to go out West, I strongly encourage you to include Yellowstone National Park on your itinerary. You'll find some of the most amazing dis-plays of God's creative glory there. One of these displays is the popular Old Faithful Geyser, which earned its name back in 1870 because of its punctual, predictable eruptions. Frequently right on time at 91-minute interval eruptions, this amazing creative work of God is seldom late. Old Faithful truly is "faithful" in showing up on time.*

In the Christian's life, things are much the same. You see, there is no "late" in the faith realm. Everything is always on time. Just as we can expect Old Faithful to erupt on schedule, we can expect God's timing in our lives to be perfectly punctual. He is always on time. And not just on time, but *right* on time—down to the second.

---

* <http://www.nps.gov/yell/tours/oldfaithful/oldfaith.htm> (15 June 2004)

DAY THIRTY-EIGHT

Faith is rewarded, but not always immediately—God's in charge of the "how" and the "when."

As we discussed in chapter thirty-eight, faith's fruits are always right on time. If we're walking in God's will, it doesn't matter what the situation is. When we're living by faith, we can be confident that God will reward that faith by answering our requests right on time. As Jesus said,

> *Ask, and it will be given to you; seek, and you will find; knock, and it will be opened to you. For everyone who asks receives, and he who seeks finds, and to him who knocks it will be opened.* (Matthew 7:7–8)

God answers prayer, and He is always on time!

Unfortunately, some people overlook an important detail at this point. They forget that "on time" means on time according to God's timing—not ours. Often there's a big difference between God's timing and our timing, so this is a very important point.

The Bible reminds us repeatedly that God's ways are different than our ways.

For as the heavens are higher than the earth, so are My ways higher than your ways, and My thoughts than your thoughts. (Isaiah 55:9)

As sovereign God, He sees all eternity while we're limited to our small corners of time and space. Because of His vast knowledge and understanding, He obviously knows what's best in the big scheme of things. He knows when our prayers should be answered and exactly how they should be answered. Sometimes those answers will match up with what we, in our flesh, are hoping for. Sometimes they won't.

Sometimes God delays to teach patience.

No matter what the response, however, we can be confident that it is the perfect answer for that point in time. God never fails. No matter how chaotic or disorderly life may seem, we can be confident that He is in control and working it all together for His glory and our good. As Romans 8:28 says,

We know that all things work together for good to those who love God, to those who are the called according to His purpose. (Romans 8:28)

Sometimes God delays His answers to teach us patience. Patience is one of those virtues that many people lack. I have to confess that this is true in my life. I don't really like waiting, and sometimes I want my desires provided for right away.

Because of this, I frequently ask God to increase my patience. He has helped me to see that if He chose to give

me everything I wanted immediately, I would lose the valuable lessons that can only be learned through patience. Patience proves how much I really want the blessing. If I sincerely want it badly enough, then I'll wait for it.

I am living proof of this truth. When I was sickened with cancer, my healing did not come overnight. In fact, it was a very long and drawn-out process. That process, however, taught me how to depend more on Jesus and what His Word says.

> *My brethren, count it all joy when you fall into various trials, knowing that the testing of your faith produces patience. But let patience have its perfect work, that you may be perfect and complete, lacking nothing.*
> (James 1:2–4)

Here's a question for you: If God always rewards faith in His timing, then why are there martyrs? Why would He allow His faithful followers to suffer painful, torturous deaths? Why doesn't He reward their faith by delivering them from the awful situations they are in?

Hebrews 11, the great "faith chapter," has our answer. After mentioning the victorious accounts of faithful followers such as Noah, Abraham, Moses, Rahab, and Gideon, the writer of Hebrews turns his attention to those faithful who endured suffering and pain:

> *Others were tortured, not accepting deliverance, that they might obtain a better resurrection. Still others had trial of mockings and scourgings, yes, and of chains and imprisonment. They were stoned, they were sawn in two, were tempted, were slain with the sword. They wandered about in sheepskins and goatskins, being destitute, afflicted, tormented; of whom the world was not worthy. They wandered in deserts and mountains,*

in dens and caves of the earth. And all these, having obtained a good testimony through faith, did not receive the promise, God having provided something better for us, that they should not be made perfect apart from us.
(Hebrews 11:35–40)

And all these, having obtained a good testimony through faith.... (verse 39)

So if they were so faithful, why did they suffer? If faith is always rewarded, what was the reward for these men and women? Were *"mockings,...scourgings,...chains and imprisonment"* their only reward? By no means! Look again at verse 35:

Others were tortured, not accepting deliverance, that they might obtain a better resurrection.

Did you catch that? They did not accept deliverance because they knew *"a better resurrection"* awaited them. They knew that whether their faith was rewarded now on earth or later in heaven, it would be rewarded nonetheless.

You're probably not facing martyrdom, but maybe you've seen this same principle in action in your own life. Maybe God answered a prayer a certain way that just doesn't make sense to you. You've been able to figure out the reasons behind other answers to prayers, but this one has you baffled. The fact of the matter is that you may never understand why He answered your prayer how He did and when He did—until heaven, that is.

> In heaven, we'll get to see the big picture.

Just as these men and women received their reward in heaven—the *"better resurrection"*—so too will you receive

your rewards in heaven. Often God will reward our faith while we're still here on earth—but sometimes He won't. It is in these situations that we have to remind ourselves of the *"better resurrection"* that awaits us because of Christ's sacrifice and resurrection.

If I could have you remember anything, it'd be this: Sometimes God's "on time" will not be experienced on this side of eternity. Some people might condemn us for what they see as a cop-out and accuse us of "waiting for our pie in the sky by and by." As far as I'm concerned, they are welcome to think what they want. An eternity with my Lord in heaven is one heavenly pie I want to taste! It is more than worth the wait.

Day Thirty-Nine

Faith isn't content to be still.

*Be still, and know that I am God; I will be
exalted among the nations, I will be
exalted in the earth!*
—Psalm 46:10

Today's world is always on the go. From fast-food restaurants and TV dinners to wireless laptops and cellular phones, our culture has been inundated with products and services that allow us to keep moving from one appointment to the next with little to no interruption. Everything must be done speedily, efficiently, on schedule, and with optimum effectiveness. With the popularity of the "power nap," even our times of rest are quick and goal-oriented. We are a busy people, always on the go.

Now don't get me wrong. There's nothing wrong with being fast, efficient, and effective. After all, doesn't God call us in His Word to be diligent in our tasks? Considering passages such as Proverbs 6:6–11, I'd say so:

Go to the ant, you sluggard! Consider her ways and be wise, which, having no captain, overseer or ruler, provides her supplies in the summer, and gathers her food in the harvest. How long will you slumber, O sluggard? When will you rise from your sleep? A little sleep, a little slumber, a little folding of the hands to sleep; so shall your poverty come on you like a prowler, and your need like an armed man. (Proverbs 6:6–11)

Such biblical callings to be diligent, however, do not stand alone. They're accompanied by reminders to be still, reflective, and quiet before our Lord.

Be still, and know that I am God; I will be exalted among the nations, I will be exalted in the earth!
(Psalm 46:10)

Be silent in the presence of the Lord God; for the day of the Lord is at hand, for the Lord has prepared a sacrifice; He has invited His guests. (Zephaniah 1:7)

This is something I think many in today's church have forgotten. Just like the world around us, we are always on the move. Frequently, it's church things that create this dizzying whirlwind. We're so busy rushing from one church activity to the next that we forget the reason all these discipleship groups, Bible studies, and ministry outreach groups even exist in the first place.

> Even in the church, we are always on the move.

What we need is a good dose of stillness. You see, faith is not afraid to be quiet before the Lord. Faith welcomes moments of silence, of time away from the rush and whir of our frenzied lives. Faith is content to sit quietly before the Lord, eager and expectant to hear all He has to say.

Day Thirty-Nine

We find a good biblical example of this in the book of Genesis. Before Abraham died, he called one of his most trusted servants to him and charged him with a very important task: finding a good wife for his son, Isaac. We find the account in Genesis 24:

Now Abraham was old, well advanced in age; and the Lord had blessed Abraham in all things. So Abraham said to the oldest servant of his house, who ruled over all that he had, "Please, put your hand under my thigh, and I will make you swear by the Lord, the God of heaven and the God of the earth, that you will not take a wife for my son from the daughters of the Canaanites, among whom I dwell; but you shall go to my country and to my family, and take a wife for my son Isaac."... So the servant put his hand under the thigh of Abraham his master, and swore to him concerning this matter.

(verses 1–4, 9)

The servant agreed to carry out Abraham's command, and he quickly set off for his master's homeland.

Then the servant took ten of his master's camels and departed, for all his master's goods were in his hand. And he arose and went to Mesopotamia, to the city of Nahor. And he made his camels kneel down outside the city by a well of water at evening time, the time when women go out to draw water. Then he said, "O Lord God of my master Abraham, please give me success this day, and show kindness to my master Abraham. Behold, here I stand by the well of water, and the daughters of the men of the city are coming out to draw water. Now let it be that the young woman to whom I say, 'Please let down your pitcher that I may drink,' and she says, 'Drink, and I will also give your camels a

drink'; let her be the one You have appointed for Your servant Isaac. And by this I will know that You have shown kindness to my master." (verses 10–14)

At this point, Rebekah, a beautiful and godly young woman, showed up on the scene. She seemed perfect in every way. She watered the camels, provided water for the servant, and was all around hospitable.

Right here in this story is where we get a good example of biblical silence. Instead of jumping to conclusions and assuming this *must* be the woman God had chosen, the servant *"remained silent."* He sought stillness before the Lord. He silenced his own voice and thoughts so that he could be sure to hear the Lord.

And the man, wondering at her, remained silent so as to know whether the LORD had made his journey prosperous or not. (verse 21)

In that moment of silence, the Lord must have confirmed that this was the woman, for shortly thereafter, the servant took action, showering her with gifts from Abraham—gifts fit for a bride-to-be.

But notice the order of events in this account: silence first, then action. The servant was not afraid to be still before the Lord. In fact, he knew that it was only in that stillness that he would receive an answer from the Lord.

Are you content with stillness before the Lord? Or are you so busy moving from one activity to the next that you barely have time to hear His voice?

DAY FORTY

Living the faith life is not a fad or phase.

Our nation is in the midst of a diet revolution. No matter where you go to eat these days, there's always a low-carb menu. Grocery stores have devoted entire aisles to low-carb foods, and even bookstores have separate shelves in the "health and wellness" section devoted to books on low-carb eating. With Atkins, South Beach, the Zone, and everything in between, low-carb seems to be the way to go when it comes to eating these days. Almost everyone who's presently trying to lose weight or has tried in the somewhat recent past has likely attempted the low-carb lifestyle.

Notice that I said "lifestyle," not "diet." Proponents of Atkins, South Beach, the Zone, and all the other low-carb meal plans are quick to point out that low-carb eating is not a diet; it's a lifestyle change, what they call a long-term "W.O.E.," or "way of eating." Low-carb meal plans are not intended to be "quick fixes" or "lose-weight-fast" schemes.

People who take on the low-carb lifestyle usually understand that it is precisely that—a lifestyle. They realize that they are committing to a lifetime of eating fewer and more complex carbohydrates. The low-carb plans emphasize a lifetime of commitment—not a week's worth of effort. The focus is on *attaining* a healthy weight and then *maintaining* it—not on quick-fix, overnight, yo-yo crash diets.

I'm not here to promote Atkins, South Beach, the Zone, or any of these meal programs. Doctors and nutritionists alike, however, will tell you that the focus each of these programs places on long-term, lifestyle change is healthy and good. Healthy eating should be a "way of living," not a phase we go through every few weeks or so whenever we need to undo the damage of our usual fast-food lifestyle.

The faith life needs to be much the same way. Faith is to be a lifestyle—a "W.O.L." or "way of living"—not a short-term change. Unfortunately, many people lock faith in the closet until they feel desperate for a "faith fix." As long as things are going smoothly, faith is kept out of sight. When things start to get rocky, however, faith is lugged out to do its job. Then, as soon as a status quo is reached, faith is put back on its shelf once more. Such "faith dieters" continue this cycle, day-in and day-out, never *attaining* or *maintaining* a healthy spiritual weight. Like the person who alternates between days of strict dieting and gluttonous overindulgence, such people are happy to treat faith as nothing more than a quick fix. Faith, however, is so much more.

> Faith is more than a "quick fix."

Don't be fooled into believing you are a faith person just because you exercised faith once, or even twice. It just

doesn't work like that. The faith walk is a lifestyle; it has to become habitual. When you take a bath or brush your teeth or put your clothes on each day, hopefully you don't have to think about it too much. You just *do* these things because each of these tasks is a habit. You don't *try* to brush your teeth; you just do. You don't *strive* to take a bath or shower; you just take one. And you don't *attempt* to put your clothes on; you just get dressed. Why? Because you have done each of these things so many times through the years that it feels almost abnormal if you forget to do them. They are habits. They have moved into the realm of "second nature," and your faith must do the same.

Has the faith life become second nature for you? Or are you still striving in the flesh to make things happen? You can only strive for so long. A day will come when all your efforts will earn you nothing more than misery. When you're consistently walking in faith, however, true joy will follow. And when you're consistently walking in faith, the faith habit will be formed.

Don't worry if faith doesn't come easily right now. No one ever said the Christian life would be simple! Faith is hard at times, and it probably won't seem "normal" when you first start exercising it. The more you continue walking in faith, however, the closer you'll be to developing "second nature" faith.

A habit is formed by repetition. My friend, I encourage you to develop the habit of faith. Decide now that you will choose the faith road in every moment. Commit to pursuing the walk of faith every day, every week, every month, every year. Decide that, no matter how challenging it may be to practice faith, you will still practice it anyway. As you repeatedly walk in faith, the habit will be formed. Trust me.

Do you think about each step you take? When a fish swims, does it ponder each flip of the fin? When a bird flies, does it reflect on each flap of the wing? I think we can agree that, for the most part, the answer to these questions is "no." In time, exercising your faith will be the same. You may be overly conscious and self-aware of your faith right now, just as a baby learning to walk thinks about how his legs work to move him across the room. In time, however, walking becomes second nature for that baby—and faith will behave the same for you.

Like a fish out of water is a seasoned Christian without faith. Keep up your faith walk. Stick with it, and your "second nature" faith will be close at hand.

ABOUT THE AUTHOR

Jack Coe, Jr.

E vangelist Jack Coe, Jr., is the oldest of six children born to Jack Coe, Sr., a prominent television evangelist and tent revival minister of the 1940s and '50s. As one of the best-known healing evangelists of the twentieth century, Jack Coe, Sr., left behind some pretty big shoes—which Jack Coe, Jr., wholeheartedly sought to fill when the Lord called him into full-time evangelistic work in 1986 while Coe, Jr., was in the midst of battling what doctors labeled "a deadly cancer." Within months of embracing his call, the Lord assured Coe he had been healed of the cancer. Coe and his wife, Frieda, continue to live out the "heritage of faith" that began with Jack Coe, Sr. They have conducted miracle crusades around the world, and they continue to share the gospel message with audiences everywhere they go.

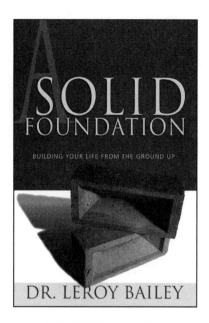

A Solid Foundation
Dr. LeRoy Bailey

When it comes to building anything of permanence and value, the need for a stable foundation is a given. Yet, when we embark upon a new business venture, start a new job, or enter into a new relationship, we're often so eager for the final results that we rush through or skip over the necessary early stages. In the end, we're left with failed businesses, unfulfilling careers, and relationships turned sour.
Dr. LeRoy Bailey reminds us that long-term success comes to those who take the necessary time to lay *A Solid Foundation* in their lives by following godly principles and a biblical blueprint. With clear, step-by-step examples, he explains how to build a sure foundation that will support the largest of life's ventures and secure enduring results.

ISBN: 0-88368-777-1 • Trade • 224 pages

ພ

WHITAKER
HOUSE

proclaiming the power of the Gospel through the written word
visit our website at www.whitakerhouse.com

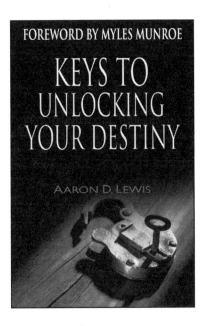

Keys to Unlocking Your Destiny
Aaron D. Lewis

You're too fat, too thin, too short, too tall, too white, or too black. You've heard it all your life....You're just not good enough! Break out of the mold that people's words have made for you, and journey toward your goals, no matter how impossible they may seem. Now is the time to fulfill the call of God upon your life and live out your purpose. Aaron D. Lewis reveals the road map to reaching your maximum potential. Your God-given destiny awaits you!

ISBN: 0-88368-720-8 • Trade • 160 pages

ЧJ
WHITAKER
HOUSE

The Believer's Handbook
Lester Sumrall

World-renowned pastor and evangelist Lester Sumrall offers straightforward answers to many of the burning questions of life, including "Who is God, and does He really care how I live my life?" He gives examples of his encounters with angels, demons, and the living God that will convince you there's more to this world than what you can experience through your senses. Discover God's perfect plan for earthly matters, too—supernatural guidance on how to live your day-to-day life. Are you ready for God to be revealed to you?

ISBN: 0-88368-852-2 • Trade • 624 pages

ແ
WHITAKER
HOUSE

proclaiming the power of the Gospel through the written word
visit our website at www.whitakerhouse.com

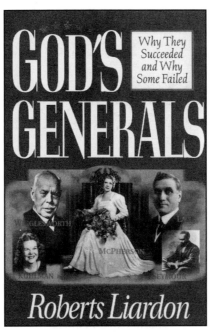

God's Generals:
Why They Succeeded and Why Some Failed
Roberts Liardon

Some of the most powerful ministers ever to ignite the fires of revival did so by dynamically demonstrating the Holy Spirit's power. In these fascinating pages, Roberts Liardon faithfully chronicles the lives and spiritual journeys of twelve of *God's Generals,* including William Seymour, the son of ex-slaves, who turned a tiny horse stable into an internationally famous revival center; Aimee Semple McPherson, the glamorous and flamboyant founder of the Foursquare Church and the nation's first Christian radio station; and Smith Wigglesworth, the plumber who read no book but the Bible—and raised the dead!

ISBN: 0-88368-944-8 • Hardcover • 416 pages

ɯ
WHITAKER
HOUSE

proclaiming the power of the Gospel through the written word
visit our website at www.whitakerhouse.com

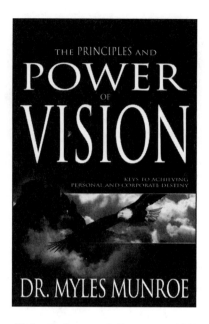

The Principles and Power of Vision
Dr. Myles Munroe

Whether you are a businessperson, a homemaker, a student, or a head of state, best-selling author Dr. Myles Munroe explains how you can make your dreams and hopes a living reality. Your success is not dependent on the state of the economy or what the job market is like. You do not need to be hindered by the limited perceptions of others or by a lack of resources. Discover time-tested principles that will enable you to fulfill your vision no matter who you are or where you come from. You were not meant for a mundane or mediocre life. Revive your passion for living, pursue your dream, discover your vision—and find your true life.

ISBN: 0-88368-951-0 • Hardcover • 240 pages

ய
WHITAKER
HOUSE

proclaiming the power of the Gospel through the written word
visit our website at www.whitakerhouse.com